Nrt-CD7

C000162276

Founder Editor: John D. Jump (1969–1976)

42 Genre

In the same series

Genre

Heather Dubrow

Methuen

London and New York

First published in 1982 by
Methuen & Co. Ltd
11 New Fetter Lane,
London EC4P 4EE

Published in the USA by
Methuen & Co.
in association with Methuen, Inc.
733 Third Avenue,
New York, NY 10017

© *1982 Heather Dubrow*

Typeset by
Scarborough Typesetting Services
and printed in Great Britain by
J. W. Arrowsmith (Bristol) Ltd

British Library
Cataloguing in Publication Data

Dubrow, Heather
Genre.—(The Critical idiom; 42)
1. Literary form
I. Title   II. Series
801'.9   PN45.5

ISBN 0–416–74680–2
ISBN 0–416–74690–X Pbk

Library of Congress
Cataloging in Publication Data

Dubrow, Heather, 1945–
Genre.
(The Critical idiom; 42)
Bibliography: p.
Includes index.
1. Literary form.   I. Title.   II. Series.
PN45.5.D8   808   82–3405

ISBN 0–416–74680–2   AACR2
ISBN 0–416–74690–X (pbk.)

To my mother and my father

Contents

Preface

This is a comparatively short book on an indubitably large topic and, like the other volumes in the Critical Idiom series, it is directed to an audience ranging from students to scholars. These conditions have made it necessary to define and delimit the scope of the book with care. My title is in the singular, not the plural: this study aims to explore general principles about genre and discusses the characteristics and the histories of particular literary forms only as they illuminate those principles. If it had alluded to every significant critical statement on genre, the book would have become a mere list of names, virtually an unannotated bibliography for the subject rather than an examination of it. I have, therefore, focused my historical discussion on a fairly small sample of theorists, selected either because they are so representative of a particular school or a particular age that studying them would be especially illuminating, or because they are so important in their own right that not studying them would be particularly unfortunate; and, though one obviously could not survey genre theory without examining classical and continental rhetoricians, I have given especial attention to the Anglo-American tradition.

In one regard, however, I have interpreted the topic of the book broadly, including examples of sub-genres, modes and some other literary types to which certain readers would deny the name genre. Adopting a more rigid definition would have demanded the exclusion of several important and intriguing forms, such as the pastoral elegy, that would definitely be called genres according to some interpretations of the term. In any event, my observations about types like these do apply with equal force to other types that all critics would agree in considering genres.

Quotations are based on the standard editions of the writers in question; in accordance with the series, however, spelling and punctuation have been modernized and documentation confined to brief references within the text.

*   *   *

Acknowledgements are, as it were, a well established sub-genre of the preface, but like many other highly conventional literary types, they can still convey genuine emotion. To begin with, I owe more debts than can be individually enumerated to the many illuminating studies of my subject that have appeared in the past few decades, especially Paul Hernadi's *Beyond Genre* and Jonathan Culler's *Structuralist Poetics*. I completed much of the work on this book while holding a Harvard University Mellon Faculty Fellowship and an Honorary American Association of University Women Fellowship, and a grant from Carleton College defrayed secretarial expenses; I wish to thank those institutions for their support. Electa Arenal and Susanne Zantop assisted me with translation. When working on this study – as on so much of my other research – I benefited greatly from the judicious advice of Herschel Baker and Maynard Mack, Jr. I am particularly indebted to Morton Bloomfield, Emerson Marks and James Wilkinson for their painstaking and perceptive readings of the entire manuscript.

The author and publisher would like to thank the following for permission to reproduce copyright material: Harvard University Press for Canzonières 189 and 190 from *Petrarch's Lyric Poems*, trans. and ed. Robert M. Durling.

1

Introduction

Most critical efforts to handle such generic terms as 'epic' or 'novel' are chiefly interesting as examples of the psychology of rumor.
(Northrop Frye, *Anatomy of Criticism*)

Assume that the following paragraph opens a novel entitled *Murder at Marplethorpe*:

> The clock on the mantelpiece said ten thirty, but someone had suggested recently that the clock was wrong. As the figure of the dead woman lay on the bed in the front room, a no less silent figure glided rapidly from the house. The only sounds to be heard were the ticking of that clock and the loud wailing of an infant.

Now read it through again, this time pretending that it appears under a title like *The Personal History of David Marplethorpe* and represents the first paragraph of a *Bildungsroman*, the narrative genre that traces the maturation and education of its hero.

In the first instance, our assumptions about detective fiction inevitably shape many of our responses. We mentally file the allusion to the clock as a clue that might later help us to identify the murderer. We interpret the inaccuracy of that clock not as a symbolic statement about time but rather as part of a game the author is playing to confound our own detective work; hence we become alert for any further clues about the peculiarities of this unreliable machine – can the person who commented on it be trusted? has anyone observed the butler tampering with it? The woman on the bed, we assume, is likely to be the victim, and the 'no less silent figure' may well be the murderer himself. Perhaps the crying of the baby merely provides an appropriately melancholy atmosphere, or perhaps it represents yet another clue (has its nursemaid abandoned it for more nefarious pursuits? has the murderer disturbed it, and, if so, what might that fact indicate about his route through the house?).

When, however, we assume that exactly the same paragraph is the opening of a *Bildungsroman*, we respond very differently. The reference to the clock once again seems to be a clue, but a clue in quite a different sense: we read that allusion symbolically, as a hint that time is disordered in the world that our novelist is evoking. In this case we become alert not for additional details about the mechanics of the clock but rather for further images of and ideas about time. We are much more likely to assume that the woman has died of natural causes. Above all, we focus far more attention, and a far different type of attention, on that noisy baby. Because the *Bildungsroman* so often opens on the birth of its central character, the possibility that the infant will be the protagonist might well flash through our minds, leading us to speculate, though perhaps subconsciously, that the dead figure is his mother and the silent one either his distraught father or an unsuccessful midwife.

What these two radically different readings reflect, of course, is the significance of literary form or genre: as we interpret the paragraph we are inevitably, though perhaps unwittingly, responding to generic signals. While certain of the problems that we will explore in this book will invite us to adduce the most arcane literary methodologies and the most abstruse literary theories, the significance of genre in the passage at hand is best clarified by an analogy from everyday life; one reason genre is so intriguing a concept is that it is related both to very specialized technical issues and to very broad human ones. One of the closest analogies to the experience of reading our hypothetical opening paragraph, then, is that of operating within a social code: genre, as many students of the subject have observed, functions much like a code of behavior established between the author and his reader. When we agree to attend a formal dinner, we tacitly accept the assumption that we will don the appropriate attire; the host in turn feels an obligation to serve a fairly elaborate meal and to accompany it with wine rather than, say, offering pizza and beer. Similarly, when we begin to read a detective novel, we agree to a willing suspension of disbelief. We may, for example, be expected to accept the unlikely proposition that our detective is gifted with quite uncanny acuteness, or that half a dozen otherwise normal people are all possessed with a motive for murder and have all gathered on the same houseboat. At the same time that it leads us to accept these improbabilities, the generic code enjoins the writer from breaking certain other laws. Were we reading a science fiction story or a Gothic tale, we would be quite prepared to believe that a murder had been committed by a ghost, but if the author of our putative *Murder at Marplethorpe* later revealed that his 'no less silent figure' was in fact a spirit, we would feel betrayed. Our annoyance would stem not from the fact that the writer had violated the laws of nature but rather that he had violated those of the code.

Generic prescriptions also resemble social codes in that they differ from culture to culture and in that they may in fact be neglected, though seldom lightly or unthinkingly. A guest may indeed choose to arrive at that dinner party sporting the most casual of clothes, but if he does so he is issuing a forceful statement about his attitudes to dress codes or even to social codes in general. If the author of a *Bildungsroman* sedulously refuses to refer to his hero's birth at the beginning of the novel, as Laurence Sterne so wittily does in *Tristram Shandy*, we are aware that he is making an important point about the *Bildungsroman* or about the type of experiences that it normally portrays.

Readers have often noted that genre invites yet another analogy from daily experience: the way a social institution, such as an established church or a legislative body, functions. It is often possible to challenge such institutions, sometimes to overthrow them, but it is virtually impossible simply to exclude them from our lives. Because so many members of the culture do accept them, an attempt to ignore them acquires intensity and resonance and begins to seem a judgment on the institution or a rebellion against it, rather than an act born of mere indifference. The man who leaves his hat on in church will often be considered actively hostile to religion; the writer who composes a sonnet about a promiscuous Dark Lady will appear not simply to be disregarding the conventional Petrarchan sonnet but rather to be flouting it, to be commenting on its dangerous inadequacies. Moreover, much like a firmly rooted institution, a well-established genre transmits certain cultural attitudes, attitudes which it is shaped by and in turn helps to shape. A school curriculum at once reflects and generates assumptions about history; the *Bildungsroman* embodies presuppositions about when and how people mature and in turn encourages its reader to see that process of maturation in the terms the novel itself has established, even when he encounters it outside the novel.

Though the effects of genre are manifest and manifold, working out a precise definition of the term can prove curiously difficult. As its etymological roots in the Latin word *genus* (kind) would suggest, 'genre' basically alludes to literary types and hence theoretically could be applied to lyric, tragedy, the novel, the sonnet, drawing-room comedy and so on. But the obvious distinctions between forms like the ones juxtaposed on that list have led a number of critics to attempt to define genre more narrowly. Many maintain that narrative, drama and lyric demand to be distinguished from types like the *Bildungsroman* and the epigram: the three forms that comprise that important triad are much broader than others, and they are further distinguished by the fact that they recur throughout Western literature. The term 'mode' is often assigned to those three literary kinds, as well as to certain others that may be said to transcend particular cultures, such as pastoral and romance; adapting the terminology of the influential German critic Karl Viëtor, some writers label such types 'universals'. At the opposite end of the scale, certain forms appear significantly narrower than the ones that we should comfortably call genres; thus it seems sensible to apply a label like 'sub-genre' to such types as drawing-room comedy, the novel of manners and the country-house poem.

Even after attempting to delimit the idea of genre in these ways, we are confronted with a large range of literary kinds whose claims to the title remain viable but debatable, depending as they do on exactly what we think a genre is and hence what characteristics we take into account when deciding whether to grant that label to a given literary type. Classical writers tended to emphasize meter as a determining factor. Accepting prosody as at least one determinant, most modern critics in England and America would call forms like the sonnet genres without hesitation; but other theorists, preferring to exclude metrical patterns from their consideration of genre, insist on placing types like the sonnet into a separate category, sometimes termed 'fixed forms'.

In any event, no one could claim that prosody is the sole determinant of genre in English literature. In some instances, it is subject matter that is decisive – witness the epithalamium, which is by definition a poem about a wedding, or the funeral elegy which is, of course, a poem about a death. When analyzing tragedy, Aristotle describes not only the subject matter appropriate to that genre but also the effect it should have on its audience – 'the plot ought to be so constructed that, even without the aid of the eye, he who hears the tale told will thrill with horror and melt to pity at what takes place' (p. 49) – and hence anticipates the emphasis many recent critics have placed on the affective qualities of genre. Thus in his study of the fantastic, Tzvetan Todorov maintains that what is central to that genre is not the subject matter *per se* but rather the state of mind it induces: an uncertainty about how the events are to be interpreted. Less tangible characteristics like attitude and tone often play a significant role too; René Wellek and Austin Warren apply the useful term 'inner form' to these qualities and in so doing distinguish them from the components of 'outer form', such as prosody.

Many genres, of course, are determined not by one of the factors we have been enumerating but rather by an interaction between

several. Its subject matter, its tone and its proclivity for certain
stanzaic patterns all figure in our definition of an ode. Nathaniel
Hawthorne's suggestive descriptions of the romance are worth
quoting at some length, for they draw attention to the subtle
amalgamation of qualities that may be said to constitute the form
in question. Among the issues he touches on are the mood, setting,
narrative techniques and subject matter that he deems appropriate
for his literary form, as well as its effects on the reader:

> When a writer calls his work a romance, it need hardly be
> observed that he wishes to claim a certain latitude, both as to its
> fashion and material, which he would not have felt himself
> entitled to assume, had he professed to be writing a novel. The
> latter form of composition is presumed to aim at a very minute
> fidelity, not merely to the possible, but to the probable and
> ordinary course of man's experience. The former − while, as a
> work of art, it must rigidly subject itself to laws, and while it sins
> unpardonably, so far as it may swerve aside from the truth of the
> human heart − has fairly a right to present that truth under
> circumstances, to a great extent, of the writer's own choosing or
> creation. If he think fit, also, he may so manage his atmos-
> pherical medium as to bring out or mellow the lights and deepen
> and enrich the shadows of the picture. . . . The point of view in
> which this tale comes under the romantic definition, lies in the
> attempt to connect a by-gone time with the very present that is
> flitting away from us. . . . When romances do really teach any-
> thing, or produce any effective operation, it is usually through a
> far more subtle process than the ostensible one.

(Preface, *The House of the Seven Gables*, pp. 1–2)

Hawthorne's pronouncements may also serve to remind us of yet
another problem that complicates the definition of genres: different literary cultures may, of course, apply the same name to
very different genres. It is not difficult to remember that the
romance as Hawthorne is defining it is not the same form as the
medieval narratives or the Renaissance dramas that bear the same

title; but the distinctions between, say, Greek and Elizabethan tragedy are at once subtle enough and significant enough to render the intrinsically hard task of defining tragedy even harder. Often, too, societies will impose different definitions on what is essentially the same genre; thus Latin poets were prone to categorize the elegy, like so many other forms, primarily in terms of its meter, while the writers who imitated that type during the English Renaissance often deviated from the prosodic patterns in their classical models and apparently considered the form to be determined instead by its subject matter and tone.

The major reason it proves so difficult to arrive at a simple and satisfactory definition of individual genres or of genre itself, then, is that the concept encompasses so many different literary qualities. Since the nineteenth century, critics have energetically pursued parallels between genres and biological species. One measure of the complexities that we have been noting and will continue to note throughout this study is that a psychological metaphor is more apt in many respects than a physiological one: I would suggest that, in the ways they are structured and the ways they function, genres are strikingly similar to human personalities. Like different personalities, different genres are distinguished from one another by which characteristics predominate: almost all poetic forms have predilections for certain prosodic patterns, just as almost all human beings have some urge to aggression, but the extent to which such tendencies are realized and their role in the total pattern of the psyche or the form in question varies tremendously. In comparing genres as in comparing different personalities, we find that various elements may assume the same function: some people express their aggressiveness by making satirical comments and others by playing team sports, while the kinds of order and repetitiveness created in one genre by an elaborate metrical pattern, may be built into other genres through, say, rhyme or narrative patterns instead.

2

The functions of genre

> It is easy to forget that the man who writes a good love sonnet needs
> not only to be enamoured of a woman, but also to be enamoured of
> the sonnet.
>
> (C. S. Lewis, *A Preface to Paradise Lost*)

Our two fictive fictions, *Murder at Marplethorpe* and *The History
of David Marplethorpe*, suggest some of the roles genre serves in
actual literary works – and in so doing indicate how much it has
affected writers and how much it can and should affect us as
readers. Since the time of romantic criticism, it has been fashion-
able to denigrate generic prescriptions by focusing on the ways
authors transmute or transcend them. Many contemporary critics
have reinforced this tendency by emphasizing the conflict between
the individual work and its literary predecessors; recent statements
on this subject range from the influential observations of Hans
Robert Jauss in his essay 'Literary history as a challenge to literary
theory' to the more extreme doctrines in Harold Bloom's *The
Anxiety of Influence*. In some important regards, of course, this
emphasis is justified: the creators of literary works, unlike the
creators of Danish Gruyère cheeses, seldom pride themselves on
the fact that their achievements are virtually indistinguishable
from the models behind them. But important though the conflict
between literary fathers and their sons, between conventional
norms and unconventional reforms may be, one needs to right the
balance, to begin a consideration of genre by stressing its significance. We should remind ourselves just how much the choice
of a particular genre influences (and, of course, is influenced by)
decisions about content, tone and form.

Established genres – whether they be popular ones like the

detective novel or serious ones like the *Bildungsroman* – carry with them a whole series of prescriptions and restrictions, some codified in the pronouncements of rhetoricians and others less officially but no less forcefully established by previous writers. However problematical the statements on tragedy in Aristotle's *Poetics* may be, there is no question but that they influenced works as diverse in their implied attitudes to tradition as Racine's *Phèdre* and Arthur Miller's *Death of a Salesman*. However differently Spenser and Herrick may interpret the moral and social significance of a wedding, the epithalamia of both poets are deeply indebted to the great Latin example of the wedding song, Catullus LXI.

These examples remind us that the respect for originality sometimes expressed by modern readers would bemuse and confuse many writers both in earlier centuries and in our own. The most distinguished authors, as well as their more mediocre contemporaries, freely adopt the plots they inherit from other writers – after all, most of the tales recounted by Chaucer's pilgrims are versions of well-known stories, and Shakespeare, like other Renaissance playwrights, bases most of his plays on plots so familiar that Ben Jonson could label one of them 'a mouldy tale'. Writers of all ages have borrowed the topoi of genres quite as frequently and quite as openly as they have borrowed plots.

The history of the epic exemplifies the force of generic conventions. Inspired by the great models that Homer created and guided by the principles that a number of rhetoricians enumerated, any poet attempting an epic writes with a deep awareness of the characteristics customarily associated with his chosen form. An epic, he recognizes, is generally a long heroic poem divided into units labelled cantos or books; its diction is elevated, its action sweeping in scope; more specific conventions include the invocation of the god or gods who will preside over the work, the roll-call of heroes, and the description of the protagonist's armor. Despite the many and manifest differences between, say, Dante's *Divina Commedia*, Spenser's *The Faerie Queene* and Byron's

Childe Harold, all of these epics are shaped by the conventions of their form.

Of course, as this list of poems alone would testify, the extent to which generic conventions are respected differs considerably from era to era and from writer to writer. Moreover, certain literary forms are associated with a great many conventions and others with only very few and very loose rules; the epic is an example, perhaps indeed the best possible example, of the first type of genre, and the novel of the second. Yet generic conventions retain considerable force even in the case of writers less intensely conscious of tradition than, say, Dante and Spenser, and in the case of genres less intimately associated with a whole host of traditions than the epic. Despite his iconoclasm even John Donne proves far more interested in traditional genres than many of his readers acknowledge; for example one of the lyrics in *The Songs and Sonets*, 'Break of Day', is clearly an *aube*, a type of love poem in which the lovers are being parted by the dawn:

> 'Tis true, 'tis day, what though it be?
> O wilt thou therefore rise from me?
> Why should we rise, because 'tis light?

> (1–3)

Donne's lesser poetry testifies to his knowledge of and his respect for many popular Renaissance genres and their conventions: numbered among those poems are instances of the verse epistle, the epigram, the epithalamium, formal verse satire and the elegy.

When an author chooses to write in a given genre, he is not merely responding to the achievements and the pronouncements of others; he himself is issuing certain statements about his art and often about art in general. The very act of adopting a literary form, especially a well-established one, implies a respect for the past, or at least for one particular period or school within it. The medieval-ism that is trumpeted in the very name of the Pre-Raphaelite Brotherhood and manifested in the style of their paintings and the subject matter of their poetry is no less evident in their repeated choice of the ballad, a genre that they believed had flourished in medieval England. While some readers dismiss Fielding's assertion that he is composing 'a comic epic-poem in prose' (Preface to *Joseph Andrews*) as a deliberately pompous joke, the phrase does serve to manifest the novelist's interest in the literature of the past and to lend respectability to the new literary form in which Fielding is writing by linking it to a far more established and far more respected form, the epic.

Decisions about meter and about stanzaic patterns often function in much the same way as ones about genre. When Pound adopts the classical metrical unit known as the sapphic in his lyric 'The Return', he is declaring his indebtedness to the achievements of the classical poets, and especially to the Greek poet, Sappho, who gave her name to this type of meter; and it is far from an accident that Pound chooses the sapphic for a poem that celebrates the renascence of the classical past. The medium is indeed the message. Other arts, too, offer suggestive analogues. François Truffaut's respect for American cinema in general and Alfred Hitchcock in particular is reflected in the way he borrows the cinematic genres associated with American film. By designing a skyscraper topped not by the customary flat roof but rather by a broken pediment, the contemporary American architect Philip Johnson paid a tribute to baroque architecture, a tribute that will be highly visible in both the literal and the figurative senses of that adjective and has already proved to be highly controversial.

As the instances of Pound and Truffaut testify, working in a genre can involve not only expressing one's indebtedness to literary tradition in general but also referring to, and glorying in, debts to particular predecessors. Pope's *Moral Essays* are so evidently based on Horace's *Sermones* that they indicate deep interest in, and even identification with, that poet. By shaping 'The Love Song of J. Alfred Prufrock' in the form of a dramatic monologue, T. S. Eliot is implicitly drawing attention to his admiration for the Victorian predecessor who pioneered that form,

Robert Browning (and by including in 'Prufrock' a few lines that parody the style and assumptions of Tennyson, Eliot effects an indirect but none the less thought-provoking comparison between Browning and Tennyson). In some cases an author chooses to underscore the esteem for a previous writer that remains implicit in a work like 'Prufrock'; when he attaches to his poem 'A Ballad of François Villon' the subtitle 'Prince of All Ballad Makers', Swinburne draws our attention to the fact that his very choice of genre expresses and embodies his regard for that medieval French poet.

*   *   *

A writer may, however, be making a statement very different from any that we have examined so far when he selects a particular genre from the multiplicity of forms open to him. Despite the Aristotelian principles that the authors of pastoral tragicomedies sometimes cited, both they and their critics were keenly aware of the ways their plays differed from established types of drama. Similarly, when Joseph Hall introduces formal verse satire into English (or at least announces that he is introducing it, since both Lodge and Donne can lay claim to the title that Hall assumes, 'the first English satirist'), he focuses as much or more attention on how unfamiliar that form is to an English audience as on how venerable its classical precedents are:

> I first adventure, with foolhardy might
> To tread the steps of perilous despight:
> I first adventure: follow me who list,
> And be the second English satirist.
> Envy waits on my back, Truth on my side;
> Envy will be my page, and Truth my guide.
>
> ('Prologue', *Virgidemiarum*, I, 1–6)

The word 'adventure' embodies the tone of the whole passage, a mood of bold and self-conscious innovation to which a verb that evokes images of heroic voyages seems very apt. For Hall as for many other writers in other genres, the choice of a literary form functions less as the willing admission of indebtedness that we have been examining so far than as a proud assertion of originality. Selecting a literary form that is not currently popular can constitute a ringing statement that one is condemning and contemning much of the literature created by one's contemporaries and one's predecessors and offering something very different in its stead.

If writing in a form that is not in vogue is a way of distinguishing oneself from the dominant literary culture of one's age, it can also be a way of aligning oneself with a subculture, with the rebellious sons who are challenging the authoritarian fathers. It is no accident that those formal verse satires numbered among their authors several of the iconoclastic young men studying law at the Inns of Court. That milieu often functioned more as a tightly knit social club than a scholarly community, and writing formal verse satires rather than love poetry or the dominant type of satire in Elizabethan England (the beast fable) was an obvious way of asserting and establishing a literary current in opposition to the main one of the period.

If, then, working in a genre sometimes resembles following the established rules of the language, at other points it is like choosing to speak slang: the process of writing in a form that is not currently established, like that of spicing one's vocabulary with slang expressions, both helps to create and helps to define an in-group. Those who write in such a genre, like those who speak slang, may discover that, with the passage of time, that same act comes to have very different connotations. The literary form in question may soon be integrated into the established poetics, just as the speech mannerisms of a sub-group may be picked up by the culture at large, and in both instances one central function of the behavior in question, distinguishing oneself from the dominant culture and asserting one's allegiance to the subculture, will be lost.

But even when writing in an established genre an author may well be making a significant statement about the ways his attitudes and the art they shape differ from the attitudes and the art of the past: a poem that fits comfortably into the most conventional of genres is often as much a declaration of independence, aesthetic and intellectual, as it is a declaration of indebtedness. However detailed the conventions associated with a literary form may be, they represent not merely an injunction to adopt certain topoi but also an invitation to adapt those topoi to the aesthetic and social conditions of one's age and to the predispositions of one's own temperament. As Claudio Guillén puts it, 'a genre is not, of course, a novel, any more than the equine species is a horse. A genre is . . . an invitation to the actual writing of a work' (*Literature as System*, p. 72). He also offers a suggestive image for the relationship between generic norms and the practice of a writer:

> A ship crosses the straits in the night and is determining its course with the help of two powerful light beams which accompany it from the heights with their rays. The light beams do not interfere with the navigator's freedom to maneuver; on the contrary, they presuppose and even favor it. The beams reach the boat's position but do not coincide with it. To whom would it occur to maintain that the direction followed by the boat 'is' one of the beams? Or that the exact point of destination 'is' one of the lights that guide it?

('Sátira y poética en Garcilaso', *Homenaje a Casalduero*, p. 232)

*　　*　　*

Perhaps it is the sonnet that provides the most intriguing examples of the merger of generic traditions and individual predilections that results when the individual work intersects with the 'beams' of generic norms. Even a few examples from its long history demonstrate how subtly and how successfully its poets engage in a dialogue with earlier sonneteers. The sole failing of Laura, the lady memorialized in Petrarch's sonnets, is her unfeeling disregard of her lover's pains, an attitude most obviously manifested in her chastity; but the poet-lover often expresses a grudging respect for even that chastity. Shakespeare, however, composes a series of sonnets about a lady who does not deserve her lover's — or more to the point, her lovers' — devotion. What she merits is only the contempt voiced in the bitter couplet, 'For I have sworn thee fair, and thought thee bright / Who art as black as hell, as dark as night' (Sonnet 147, 13–14).

Several poems in Shakespeare's sequence explicitly contrast an older and purer world, 'those holy antique hours' (Sonnet 68, 9) when true love could survive and even thrive, with the contemporary world, a city of endless night inhabited by corrupt and corrupting lovers like his Dark Lady. Similarly, by the very act of adopting Petrarch's genre, Shakespeare is implicitly inviting us to compare his vision of love with that of his predecessor, to perceive and to ponder on the differences in the emotions they are conveying. Form is mirroring content, as it so often does in this sequence. But the comparisons Shakespeare effects between his own world and Petrarch's are double-edged. If the contrast with a more traditional sequence evidently serves to denigrate Shakespeare's dark world and the Dark Lady who inhabits it while glorifying Laura and the values she embodies, it also carries with it a criticism of Petrarch and his genre: in using Petrarchan conceits to describe behavior that hardly conforms to Petrarchan codes, he raises the disturbing possibility that perhaps even poets who write more conventional sonnets are lying about the nature of love. This undercurrent becomes overt in Sonnet 94 ('They that have pow'r to hurt, and will do none'), among whose complexities is an attack on the traditional Petrarchan mistress. And at one point in the sequence Shakespeare mocks another aspect of Petrarchism, its reliance on clichés:

> My mistress' eyes are nothing like the sun—
> Coral is far more red than her lips' red—
> If snow be white, why then her breasts are dun—
> If hairs be wires, black wires grow on her head:
>
> (Sonnet 130, 1–4)

Yet Shakespeare's speaker elsewhere uses Petrarchan language no less hackneyed than the phrases he so effectively parodies in Sonnet 130. The diction of Sonnets 140 and 141, for example, could have been lifted from a miscellany of the most conventional Renaissance sonnets: 'Be wise as thou art cruel' (Sonnet 140, 1), 'my pity-wanting pain' (Sonnet 140, 4), 'thy proud heart's slave and vassal wretch' (Sonnet 141, 12). The explanation of this paradox is probably neither that these two poems are artistic failures nor, as some readers have maintained, that they are early works slotted into the sequence. Rather, Shakespeare is demonstrating that his speaker, much like Sidney's Astrophil, cannot escape the poetic faults he can diagnose in others, a weakness paralleled by the way he is unable to avoid the moral failings he recognizes so clearly in the Friend and Dark Lady.

Wordsworth, too, frequently comments on earlier sonnets and sonneteers, but he does so in a very different way and to very different ends. When he laments the current political situation and declares the need for another leader like Milton, it is the sonnet form that he chooses:

London, 1802

MILTON! thou shouldst be living at this hour:
England hath need of thee: she is a fen
Of stagnant waters: altar, sword, and pen,
Fireside, the heroic wealth of hall and bower,
Have forfeited their ancient English dower
Of inward happiness. We are selfish men;
Oh! raise us up, return to us again;
And give us manners, virtue, freedom, power.
Thy soul was like a star, and dwelt apart;
Thou hadst a voice whose sound was like the sea:
Pure as the naked heavens, majestic, free,
So didst thou travel on life's common way,
In cheerful godliness; and yet thy heart
The lowliest duties on herself did lay.

By casting his complaint in the mold of a sonnet, he is aligning himself with the long tradition of poets who had used the same form to issue political statements, a company that of course includes among its many members Milton and Petrarch. There is also a hint, perhaps, that in adopting the genre that Milton himself had employed to deliver laments similar to those Milton himself has uttered, Wordsworth is attempting to fill the very need he is describing, to assume some of Milton's responsibilities as prophet and social critic.

The sonnet enjoyed a considerable vogue in the Victorian period with such writers as Elizabeth Barrett Browning and Dante Gabriel Rossetti contributing to the tradition. The nineteenth-century novelist and poet George Meredith also experiments with sonnet conventions and, by entitling his sequence *Modern Love*, he too invites us to compare his work with Renaissance sonnets − but unlike many of his contemporaries he approaches the genre with marked detachment and ambivalence.

The most striking difference between Meredith's sequence of love poems and earlier ones is the very situation from which *Modern Love* springs. For not the least of its ironies is that the speaker has in a sense attained precisely what his predecessors in the tradition desired in vain: far from rejecting him, as Petrarchan mistresses were prone to do, his lady has married him, and when the sequence opens they are actually in bed. But he has achieved all this only to suffer no less misery than his counterparts in Renaissance sonnet sequences.

Juxtaposing the opening poem in *Modern Love*, which employs the common Petrarchan image of a stone-like mistress, with a more conventional rendition of that conceit clarifies other distinctions between Meredith's poems and the tradition behind them:

> Do I not see that fairest images
> Of hardest marble are of purpose made?
> For that they should endure through many ages,
> Ne let their famous monuments to fade.

Why then do I, untrained in lovers' trade,
Her hardness blame, which I should more commend?

(Spenser, *Amoretti*, Sonnet 51, 1–6)

By this he knew she wept with waking eyes:
That, at his hand's light quiver by her head,
The strange low sobs that shook their common bed,
Were called into her with a sharp surprise,
And strangled mute, like little gaping snakes,
Dreadfully venomous to him. She lay
Stone-still, . . .

       they from head to feet
Were moveless looking through their dead black years,
By vain regret scrawled over the blank wall.
Like sculptured effigies they might be seen
Upon their marriage-tomb, the sword between;
Each wishing for the sword that severs all.

(*Modern Love*, Sonnet 1, 1–7, 11–16)

In Spenser's version, the lady's stoniness represents her virtuous disdain; in Meredith's, the image suggests a lack of communication and lack of love. It is telling, too, that in developing the image Meredith proceeds to compare both lovers to stone effigies, while in traditional Petrarchan sonnets very distinct figures of speech are generally associated with the mistress and her poet-lover respectively. The similar way Meredith's husband and wife are described in this poem prepares us for the similar way they act later in the sequence: rather than evoking a disdainful lady and her pining lover, Meredith presents a man and woman both of whom are overwhelmed by their unruly feelings and impulses. The imagery of death associated with stone here foreshadows the price they will pay for their irrationality.

One function of Meredith's many allusions to the sonnet tradition is, as some readers have suggested, to underscore the disparity between the corrupted love he depicts and the purer emotion often associated with that genre. But Meredith, like Shakespeare, is ambivalent about the sonnet and the values it represents: he keeps reminding us that the conventions of this and other literary forms are themselves a dangerous game, an aesthetic analogue to the social games and artifices in which his lovers engage. Competing and conflicting visions jar with the elements of sonnet, pastoral and romance that are woven into *Modern Love,* much as snakes lurk beneath the surface of the seemingly peaceful social situations some of the poems evoke.

Meredith's prosody expresses in microcosm his complex attitudes towards the sonnet. For the lyrics in *Modern Love* are constructed out of the unit used in the octave of a Petrarchan sonnet – the quatrain *abba* – but Meredith's poems consist of four of those quatrains and hence signally lack one of the basic determinants of a sonnet, a fourteen-line stanza. Encouraged by the fact that the term could be used loosely in Renaissance England and emboldened by the knowledge that Meredith himself twice applied it to *Modern Love,* some critics have unapologetically called the poems sonnets. This is misleading. In the nineteenth century, after all, that title was generally reserved for fourteen-line poems; and in context Meredith's own use of the word does not preclude the possibility that he is playing on the genre rather than writing within it. Just as misleading, however, is the critical tendency to underestimate the many ways Meredith's sequence is in fact related to the sonnet.

Instead, we should acknowledge that he is expressing his own and his speaker's ambivalence about the assumptions behind that genre by writing in a form that itself bears so ambivalent a relationship to the sonnet's prosody. That emotionally disturbed speaker cannot or will not write sonnets in the precise sense of the term any more than he will wholeheartedly take on the role with which he occasionally flirts, the respectful poet-lover. In more subtle ways as well, the stanza he uses mirrors his relationship to traditional sequences and traditional attitudes to love. The fact that his form is prosodically far simpler than sonnets normally are is a measure of the speaker's desire to oversimplify human experience. It is suggestive, too, that for all their psychological turmoil, sonnet speakers are sometimes able to achieve the comforting, objective generalizations that in the Shakespearean sonnet are expressed and symbolized by the couplet, or alternatively the logical movement from cause to effect, from thesis to antithesis that can be involved in the octet-sestet division of the Petrarchan sonnet. A stanza of four quatrains, in contrast, lacks these types of decisiveness and progression. By choosing a form so repetitive, Meredith is echoing prosodically the very sense of entrapment, of effigy-like stasis, that his lovers suffer.

A number of twentieth-century poets write sonnets that might borrow the title *Modern Love* from Meredith because, while adopting several characteristics of conventional sonnet sequences, they also invite us to compare their more cynical visions with the idealism of many earlier poems in their genre. In the sequence published as *Berryman's Sonnets*, the American poet John Berryman repeatedly highlights that contrast by incorporating into his poems brief echoes of Renaissance sonnets and by playing the formal and highly stylized stanzaic pattern of his genre against contemporary colloquialisms ('Is it possible, poor kids, you must not come out?' (Sonnet 87, 1)). The conflict between generic norms and expectations on the one hand and his own vision of love on the other is also enacted on the levels of diction and syntax themselves, for there Berryman frequently yokes together two disparates, juxtaposing in close conjunction a formal, high style reminiscent of older sonnets with his self-consciously modern, colloquial usages:

> Presently the sun
> yellowed the pines & my lady came not
> in blue jeans & a sweater.

> (Sonnet 115, 12–14)

At one point the poet comments on earlier works in his genre more extensively and more explicitly; as Wyatt and Spenser before

him had done, he composes a poem in imitation of Petrarch's
Canzonière 189:

> Passa la nave mia colma d'oblio
> per aspro mare a mezza notte il verno
> enfra Scilla et Caribdi, et al governo
> siede 'l signore anzi 'l nimico mio;
> à ciascun remo un penser pronto et rio
> che la tempesta e 'l fin par ch' abbi a scherno;

[My ship laden with forgetfulness passes through a harsh sea, at
midnight, in winter, between Scylla and Charybdis, and at the
helm sits my lord, rather my enemy. Each oar is manned by a
ready, cruel thought that seems to scorn the tempest and the
end; a wet, changeless wind of sighs, hopes, and desires breaks
the sail;]

(Petrarch, Canzonière 189, 1–6)

> What was Ashore, then? . . . Cargoed with Forget,
> My ships runs down a midnight winter storm
> Between whirlpool and rock, and my white love's form
> Gleams at the wheel, her hair streams. When we met
> Seaward, Thought frank & guilty to each oar set
> Hands careless of port as of the waters' harm.

(Berryman, Sonnet 15, 1–6)

Not an allegorical and abstract personification of Love but rather
the beloved herself sits at the helm, the description of her gleaming
body and streaming hair suggesting at once a desirable woman and
a dangerous phantasm. If this alteration renders the poem more
immediate, it also renders it more bitter and disturbing. Rather
than being the victims of an allegorized and externalized lord, the
lovers have no one but themselves to blame. And rather than
functioning merely as the object of the poet's desires, the woman is
characterized by a sexuality that is appealing but also evidently
destructive. The allusion to her whiteness, emphasized by the

unusual placement of the adjective, operates ironically, for Petrarch's Laura is repeatedly associated with that color to signify her chastity, while here the color reflects the speaker's desire for a body that he has come to know very well.

Another major change from earlier versions of the poem is announced by the opening four words. Petrarch and Wyatt had both referred to a port in their concluding lines without introducing the allusion earlier; Berryman expands the idea of a world elsewhere by opening with the phrase 'What was Ashore, then?' and by alluding to the port in the sixth as well as the closing line. The world of the shore in a sense represents security, but since the poet stresses throughout that he is chronicling an adulterous love, it could also refer to his marriage – a reading that gives extra resonance to the despair about returning to port on which the poem concludes.

Berryman appends the parenthetical phrase 'After Petrarch and Wyatt' to his poem. On one level his meaning is obvious: the preposition may merely be glossed as 'in imitation of'. But the word also contains a hint of a temporal dimension, of its customary denotation 'at a later period': throughout this sonnet and throughout the sequence in which it figures, the American poet is suggesting, much as Shakespeare before him had done, that he is writing of a world that has succeeded the earlier, purer one inhabited by at least some of his predecessors in the genre.

The one balanced and harmonious relationship present in sequences like the ones we have been examining is not a personal relationship described by the sonneteers but rather an aesthetic one enacted by their poems – that of form and content. Frequent and telling though their allusions to earlier sonnets may be, these poets are not, as it were, merely referring back to art for art's sake: their comments on previous sonneteers exemplify and extend the ideas above love that they are exploring throughout their sequences. Reacting against their predecessors' acceptance of Aristotle's *mimesis* (the doctrine that art exists to present a replica of the world), modern critics sometimes go too far in the opposite direction, reading art as only a comment on itself. Even the sonnet, perhaps the most self-conscious and self-referential of all genres, can demonstrate the danger of that approach.

As these instances from the history of the sonnet demonstrate, the 'invitation to form' that Claudio Guillén describes often becomes, as it were, an invitation to reformulate and an invitation to reform. In other words, one motive for writing in a genre is the urge to question some of the underlying attitudes that shape that literary mode. *Sir Gawain and the Green Knight,* for instance, is firmly rooted in the traditions of the medieval romance. Among the many characteristics that link the plot of this poem with those of more conventional works in the genre are the challenge from a threatening adversary and the resulting heroic quest; and its author evidently delights in a number of the other conventions of his form, such as the lengthy description of the hero's armor. Yet the anonymous author of this romance feels towards certain assumptions of his genre no less contempt than his hero experiences for the lady who deceives him. The poet's doubts about the ethical values behind the romance and about the genre that embodies and reflects those values are manifested in the way he twists some of the conventions of his literary form and ignores or downplays others. Thus the allusion to the battles that Gawain fights on his way to Bercilak's castle is tossed in so off-handedly,

> Now with serpents he wars, now with savage wolves,
> Now with wild men of the woods, that watched from the
>   rocks,
> Both with bulls and with bears, and with boars besides
>
> (720-2)

that one may suspect that the poet is implicitly mocking the grandiose accounts of heroic deeds around which the romance is so often structured. Killing the odd ogre, he is suggesting, is really worth only half a line. A student production at Harvard in the autumn of 1979 made the same point through clever stagecraft. The narrator informed us 'He climbed over cliffs in many strange lands', at which point the vast cliffs, represented by stagehands holding sheets, collapsed to nothing at the mere touch of Gawain's foot. The crumpled mountains offered an emblem of our hero's ability to surmount obstacles, while at the same time guying the literary tradition that repeatedly suggests that craggy mountains and horrendous monsters can be so readily vanquished.

The implication behind the treatment of Gawain's conquests is writ large in the poem as a whole. *Sir Gawain and the Green Knight* offers wry insights into courtly love and courtly honor, insights that call into question a society that accepts those values uncritically or a genre that lauds them unthinkingly. Bercilak's wife attempts to use the rules of courtly love to seduce Gawain and in the process manifests not only her own moral limitations but also the moral dangers inherent in the rules. Both Gawain and the reader come to see the purity on which he had prided himself as not only unattainable but also undesirable in its priggishness; like another perfectionist, Overdo in *Bartholomew Fair*, he learns that he must say he is Adam, flesh and blood, and forget his other name of Overdo. Even (or especially) the heroism that romances customarily laud is held up to scrutiny; the reader comes to share Bercilak's contention that Gawain should not feel so much shame when he flinches from a blow. In place of that heroism the author of this extraordinary poem substitutes another value, the ability to face one's mistakes and one's limitations no less bravely than Gawain and the heroes in more traditional romances faced all those ogres.

It is often assumed that the generic parody involved in, say, Pope's mock heroic poem *The Rape of the Lock* or in the burlesque sonnets fashioned by the sixteenth-century poet John Davies represents an entirely different phenomenon from the kinds of literary imitation that we have been examining so far; the act of writing within a genre and the act of parodying it are seen as two totally different responses to the literature of the past. The truth, however, is more complex and, indeed, more intriguing. The decision to parody a genre at the very least indicates some involvement with its values, some interest in what previous writers have achieved in it. Davies is still enough of an Elizabethan to want to parody that characteristic Elizabethan form, the love sonnet; while Rochester, writing several generations later, probably had no less contempt than Davies for the distorted language and the distorted attitudes towards love that sonnets often contained, he felt too distant from that form to bother to parody it. A writer may even have real respect for assumptions behind the literary type that he is parodying. Pope's *The Rape of the Lock* on one level mocks heroism by deflating it – by exposing the grand as merely grandiose – but on another level the poem focuses not on inherent limitations in heroic ideals and the literature that celebrates them but rather on the ways Augustan England is travestying those potentially admirable values.

Most important, the fact that works parodying a genre may well include criticism of its stylistic mannerisms and ethical concerns does not constitute as radical a distinction between these works and the 'straight' versions of the same literary form as most readers have supposed. Often the difference is one of degree rather than of kind: as we have seen, works within a given genre frequently include some re-evaluations and revisions of its conventions while works that parody the genre may simply criticize its conventions more systematically and more severely. Or the difference may be one of method: sometimes writings within a genre call its assumptions into question by omitting or twisting generic conventions while the parodic version burlesques them. The author of *Sir Gawain and the Green Knight* is no less dubious about certain elements of the romance than Davies is about certain elements of the mode that he is mocking, but the medieval poet exposes the limitations of his genre by contrasting some of its conventions with the psychological realities he is exploring, while Davies often invokes in exaggerated form the conventions for which he has least respect. The literary imitation of earlier works in a genre and the literary parody of them represent, then, not polar opposites but rather two ends of a spectrum.

Another way a writer may use a genre to comment on moral values is by playing off one literary form against another. By juxtaposing *The Knight's Tale*, a medieval romance, with *The Miller's Tale*, which recounts a strikingly similar plot from the strikingly different perspective of the fabliau, Chaucer encourages us to compare not only those tales *per se* but also the fundamental attitudes that shape their two genres. Characteristically, he invites a balanced perspective rather than simplistic judgments: we come to see that both the refined idealism of the story that the Knight tells and the crude cynicism of the Miller's narrative are wanting, and yet we also come to realize that each perspective provides a useful corrective to the other.

Writers may also incorporate an allusion to or a brief episode in one literary genre within a work based primarily on another mode. While some readers would maintain that on the heath Lear undergoes the typical pastoral experience of regeneration, though in an atypically violent form, it seems more likely that what we are encountering in that scene is a disturbing version of anti-pastoral. The scene, and of course the play as a whole, invokes many traditional pastoral concerns (the difference between man in society and the 'poor, bare, forked animal' (III, iv, 110) that he becomes in the wilderness, the balance between kindness and cruelty in human nature and so on). One reason these pastoral themes are introduced is to keep our memories of pastoral very active − not to comfort us but rather to remind us that the values celebrated in conventional pastoral literature are inaccessible in a universe like Lear's, a universe in which both human and physical nature are terrifyingly unnatural.

Marlowe's *The Jew of Malta*, a play whose own genre is variously classified as tragedy, comedy and farce, includes a number of scenes that appear to come from a literary form very different from that of the play as a whole. As many readers have observed, the episode in which Barabas awaits his daughter, Abigail, as she attempts to steal his treasure from a nunnery sounds surprisingly like a love scene in a romantic comedy:

Barabas. O my girl,
  My gold, my fortune, my felicity,

Strength to my soul, death to mine enemy.
Welcome, the first beginner of my bliss!
O Abigail, that I had thee here too,
Then my desires were fully satisfied;
But I will practise thy enlargement thence.
O girl, O gold, O beauty, O my bliss!
Abigail. Father, it draweth towards midnight now,
And 'bout this time the nuns begin to wake;
To shun suspicion, therefore, let us part.
Barabas. Farewell, my joy, and by my fingers take
A kiss from him that sends it from his soul.

(II, i, 47–59)

Marlowe is incorporating this echo of a very different sort of play in order to remind us how inappropriate its optimistic and often sentimental attitudes are in a world that in fact includes fools and knaves like the ones who populate Malta. Romantic love seems laughable, or worse, dangerous, in a universe where all emotion can be manipulated for sinister ends, as Ferneze's love for Abigail will be later in the play, or shown up as hypocritical, as the pious truisms of the rulers of Malta are. But readers generally ignore the fact that this brief glimpse of a different genre and hence a different set of values and assumptions in fact provides a kind of double-edged satire: just as *The Rape of the Lock* reflects its author's regret that his society cannot live up to what is genuinely impressive in heroic ideals, so this passage in *The Jew of Malta* hints at a faint but lingering regret that the gentler emotions of romantic comedy are totally inaccessible in Malta.

Later in the play Marlowe teases us – and teaches us – by providing a false ending, yet another illusion in a play that both studies and embodies deceit of all sorts:

Officer. Dead, my lord, and here they bring his body.
   [Enter Officers, carrying Barabas as dead.]
Del Bosco. This sudden death of his is very strange.

Ferneze. Wonder not at it, sir, the heavens are just:
Their deaths were like their lives; then think not of 'em.
Since they are dead, let them be buried.
For the Jew's body, throw that o'er the walls,
To be a prey for vultures and wild beasts.
So, now away, and fortify the town.

(V, i, 53–60)

But Barabas is not in fact dead, and the play is not in fact over:

Barabas. What, all alone? well fare, sleepy drink.
I'll be reveng'd on this accursed town,

(V, i, 61–2)

The reason the audience is fooled by the false ending is that this is
exactly the way a play of another but related literary type, the *de
casibus* tragedy, would end. In plays of that type, we witness the
rise and fall of a hero, frequently one who has overreached himself
through dangerous ambition. The moral implications of his fall
are often spelled out in a dogmatic speech very like the one
Ferneze delivers here.

By bringing into play our memories of works in the *de casibus*
tradition, Marlowe is inviting us to compare the pat morality of
such drama with his own very different and very disturbing vision.
Rosalie Colie's suggestive observation that Shakespeare often
turns his commentary on literary forms into a commentary on
moral assumptions (*Shakespeare's Living Art*, pp. 26ff.) also
describes the practice of Marlowe and, of course, of so many other
writers as well.

If, then, we try to classify *The Jew of Malta* generically, we find
that, like a number of other works, it relates to generic norms in
much the same way actual physical objects may relate to the color
spectrum: no one genre, no one hue appears in isolation, and none
appears in its purest state. For a particular work of art may con-
form to a single, clearcut generic pattern and in so doing resemble,
as it were, a primary color. Or it may participate in a genre like

pastoral romance that is in fact a combination of literary forms, much as the secondary colors − orange, green, violet − are mixtures of adjacent hues. Or it may move between distinguishable but related genres as, say, *The Faerie Queene* does, and hence remind us of intermediate colors like yellow-green. But certain works, such as *The Jew of Malta*, dazzle and disturb us with a kaleidoscopic array of hues in which it is difficult to discern a dominant one, a single genre with whose name we can confidently label the work. (Genre may be fruitfully compared to the color spectrum in many other regards as well. Much as colors appear in actual objects in different degrees of saturation, for example, so a work may display the characteristics of its genre vividly and precisely or, alternatively, offer an altered and less vivid version of generic patterns. And in a sense the opposing and paired genres that Claudio Guillén has termed 'genre and counter-genre', such as pastoral and satire, resemble complementary colors − when combined they complete a spectrum of human emotions and values.)

Often the Chinese-box arrangement of genre within genre that we observed in *The Jew of Malta* is a reflection of a pattern writ large in the literary system of the period: frequently when two forms assume the relationship of genre and counter-genre they enact their dialogue within poems of either genre as well as in the larger literary culture. Pastoral and satire are again a case in point; the inclusion of satirical passages within pastoral elegies (notably 'Lycidas', the one we will examine) should be seen not as an isolated and idiosyncratic phenomenon but rather as yet another instance of the affinity these two forms have for each other. Pastoral and epic are also prone to assume such a relationship. Epics characteristically incorporate an episode in which the hero temporarily abandons his quest in favor of a pastoral idyll or a relationship with a temptress that mirrors many pastoral motifs without overtly participating in that mode; in turn, pastorals not infrequently encompass reminders of the epic world.

The very act of choosing a genre, then, involves making a number of implicit statements about one's reactions to that mode of literature, to the other writers who have adopted it and to the cultures that have respected it. The genre in which the writer is working may come to represent the literature of the past in general, the achievements and the attitudes of a particular author whose writing typifies that genre or the values that it customarily upholds.

In addition to establishing his attitudes to the writers of the past and their work, an author may use his selection of a genre as a signal, or even a command, to contemporary writers and to those who will succeed him. The choice of one literary form over another can constitute a ringing affirmation that the genre in question is particularly appropriate for its age and possibly for succeeding ones as well, that the poem currently being written can and should serve as a model to be imitated. Hall makes this injunction explicit in the passage that I quoted above: 'Follow me who list, / And be the second English satirist.' Similarly, Alain Robbe-Grillet's experimental novel *Les Gommes* reinterprets the classic detective novel, a form that intrigued him, in order to make a statement about aesthetic principles. Loosely basing his plot on the Oedipus legend, he creates a story in which the motives for the murder and the identity of the murderer are deliberately obscured throughout, a story whose confusions and ambiguities are heightened rather than resolved at the end. In so doing Robbe-Grillet is implicitly urging contemporary and future writers to join him in questioning the basic assumptions behind more traditional novels, notably the notions that people operate from comprehensible motives and that experience forms a neat enough pattern to permit novels to have a clearcut beginning, middle and end. The essays in Robbe-Grillet's *Pour un nouveau roman* in effect constitute a manifesto directing writers to reshape the narrative modes of the past; by reshaping the detective novel as he does, Robbe-Grillet issues the same command more indirectly but no less powerfully. In other words, writing in a genre can be a highly polemical gesture, a way of attempting to initiate a new chapter of literary history through the act of creating a single work of art.

*   *   *

E. D. Hirsch writes, 'A genre is less like a game than like a code of social behavior' (*Validity in Interpretation*, p. 93). As we have already seen, this important statement has a number of implications, not the least of which is that a genre represents not only a pronouncement that a writer is making to and about the writers of the past, not only an injunction that he is delivering to the authors who may follow in his footsteps, but also a communication from the writer to his readers. He is in effect telling us the name and rules of his code, rules that affect not only how he should write the work but also how we should read it.

The establishment of a prosodic pattern, an activity that has been described as the creation of a 'metrical contract' between author and reader, offers a useful comparison. By setting up a certain meter in the first few lines of his poem, the poet teaches us what to expect and what to respond to as the work progresses. In the poems in which Yeats establishes a four-stress meter, we learn, without perhaps consciously realizing that we have done so, that the number of unstressed syllables will not be worth noticing. When, on the other hand, he writes in accentual-syllabic verse, we recognize that the alternations of stressed and unstressed syllables are well worth noticing, that deviations from, say, an iambic pattern will signal and indeed help to create important shifts in mood. Using this analogy with meter, the way genre establishes a relationship between author and reader might fruitfully be labelled a generic contract. Through such signals as the title, the meter and the incorporation of familiar topoi into his opening lines, the poet sets up such a contract with us. He in effect agrees that he will follow at least some of the patterns and conventions we associate with the genre or genres in which he is writing, and we in turn agree that we will pay close attention to certain aspects of his work while realizing that others, because of the nature of the genres, are likely to be far less important.

We know *The Comedy of Errors* is, as its very title announces, comedic, and thus we do not take the threats of death in the opening scene seriously. Rather than being distracted by fears for the well-being of the characters, we remain free to focus on the most important and most delightful element in the play, the convolutions of the plot. Though Theseus threatens Hermia with death, we never for a moment believe that *A Midsummer Night's Dream* will culminate in a heart-rending portrayal of her execution: we know that comedies customarily end on marriage rather than death, and a few minutes before Theseus delivers his threat to Hermia, he and Hippolyta signal the genre of the play by talking of their impending marriage. (As that dialogue between Theseus and Hippolyta reminds us, scenes of exposition may provide not only the background information we will require to understand the play but also the signs we will need to recognize its genre.) In much the same way, the violence with which the protagonist in Charlie Chaplin movies is so often threatened does not alarm us; one rule of the code, one assumption behind the genre, is that no one will get seriously hurt. The structuralists have suggested that one of the most illuminating ways to analyze plots is to enumerate some of the events that cannot happen in them; the same point might be made about analyzing genres. In any event, in all of these instances, whether literary or cinematic, our knowledge of the generic contract allows us to maintain the appropriate mood and to concentrate on what is most significant about the work.

Since popular literature plays by the rules far more regularly and reliably than serious literature, it provides an even clearer example of how generic expectations may still the turbulent emotions a reader might otherwise experience. Kenneth Burke suggests in *Attitudes toward History* that genres provide 'frames of acceptance' (pp. 43ff.); though he does not explore the point in relationship to popular genres, it can be adapted to apply to them as well as to the more serious literary forms he discusses. If a murderer appeared in a serious novel and threatened the life of the hero, we would experience infinitely more fear than if we learned that the villain we encountered in the opening of *Murder at Marplethorpe* were plotting against our detective hero; one reason, of course, is that the characters in a *Bildungsroman* are often better realized than those in a popular genre, but an even more fundamental reason is that detective novels tend to adhere closely to their conventions, which rule out the death of our hero. We can go a step further and recognize that it is no accident that the most popular of genres show a predilection for the most violent of events – the murders in detective fiction and spy thrillers are the most obvious modern instances, but one could also adduce the uncanny happenings in Victorian ghost stories or those in Gothic novels. Nor is the nature of the violence an accident. What occurs is often an event that members of the society fear very much, or a transmutation of such an event onto a level where they will recognize it subconsciously but perhaps not consciously: the thriller evidently speaks to our acknowledged fears of criminals and enemy agents, the popular-ized nineteenth-century American romance contains instances of miscegenation, while Victorian ghost stories sometimes include sexually promiscuous or lesbian women. Cinematic versions of popular genres also offer analogues: the children in movies about demonic possession turn on their parents in what is essentially an exaggerated version of the way many parents fear their troubled offspring are now behaving, or may soon behave. We might find it humiliating to express under other circumstances our fear of such occurrences; perhaps we might also hesitate to express such fear lest it become even harder to control once it is overt. These popular forms provide us with a socially acceptable forum for acknowledging our worries.

That forum is so appealing precisely because what might other-wise be an unmanageable terror is transmuted into a pleasurable *frisson*: the rules of the genre carefully spell out what can and what cannot happen and in many instances preclude the realization of our worst fears even while permitting others to be enacted (thus we know that the criminal may commit many crimes that frighten us, but he will not harm any of the characters about whom we are most concerned and he will be safely caught at the end of the detective novel). We receive further reassurance from the fact that the very nature of the genre implies its distance from 'real life'; such narratives enact what we most fear in our lives even while in a sense reassuring us that it will not happen.

Victor Shklovsky, one of the Russian formalists, has posited the theory that literature works through a process of 'defamiliariz-ation'; that is, it makes us look anew at otherwise familiar experiences by using such devices as meter to cast those experiences in a new light. The examples from both popular and serious literature that we have been examining suggest that one way genre itself operates might be termed 'familiarization' – our recognition of a genre encourages us to relate whatever the work at hand is evoking to the experiences portrayed in other works we have read in the same genre, a process that is mirrored in the author's implicit acknowledgement of similarities between his aesthetic experiences in writing the work and those of other writers who have adopted the same form. One function of these processes in popular literature, as we have been observing, is to allow one to say the unsayable, while in more serious literature familiarization serves to signal and perhaps even to establish some sense of community among writers. Familiarization and defamiliarization are evidently not mutually contradictory; a principal function of familiarization, of course, is to create in the reader's mind a series of assumptions about the aesthetic norms of the work at hand and the human norms that it expresses, assumptions that will make the deviations from them that constitute one type of defamiliarization all the more striking.

Genre may function as a code between writer and reader in other senses as well. Like prosodic patterns, generic signals often draw attention to the fact that what we are encountering is a fiction, rather than, say, an actual transcription of a funeral oration or a conversation between lovers; *pace* Käte Hamburger, such signals often prevent us from reading a lyric as anything other than a literary utterance. Thus the 'inexpressibility conceit', in which a writer declares that it is impossible to express woe as deep as his, can help us to realize that the elegy we are reading is not a transcription of a speech delivered spontaneously at a funeral but rather an instance of the genre that so often opens on the conceit in question.

Genre may also assume a key role in conveying the very meaning of a work. The sonnet is once again a useful case in point:

Una candida cerva sopra l'erba
verde m'apparve con duo corna d'oro,
fra due riviere all'ombra d'un alloro,
levando 'l sole a la stagione acerba.
Era sua vista sì dolce superba
ch' i' lasciai per siguirla ogni lavoro,
come l'avaro che 'n cercar tesoro
con diletto l'affanno disacerba.
'Nessun mi tocchi', al bel collo d'intorno
scritto avea di diamanti et di topazi.
'Libera farmi al mio Cesare parve'.
Et era 'l sol già vòlto al mezzo giorno,
gli occhi miei stanchi di mirar, non sazi,
quand' io caddi ne l'acqua et ella sparve.

[A white doe on the green grass appeared to me, with two golden horns, between two rivers, in the shade of a laurel, when the sun was rising in the unripe season. Her look was so sweet and proud that to follow her I left every task, like the miser who as he seeks treasure sweetens his trouble with delight. 'Let no one touch me', she bore written with diamonds and topazes around her lovely neck. 'It has pleased my Caesar to make me free'. And the sun had already turned at midday; my eyes were tired by looking but not sated, when I fell into the water, and she disappeared.]

(Petrarch, Canzonière 190)

Even if we encountered this poem in isolation from the other lyrics in the Canzonière, our knowledge of genre would provide invaluable clues about how to interpret it. We know that sonnets are generally, though not invariably, concerned with love; we realize that that pursuit is often compared to a hunt; we remember that

the lover is frequently portrayed in a natural setting. A reader unfamiliar with these traditions of the sonnet, however, will almost
inevitably fall into a number of errors not only on his initial
reading of the poem but even on subsequent readings, no matter
how sensitive he may be to the nuances of Petrarch's language. His
first impression of the opening four lines might well be that the
deer is not substantially more important than other constituents of
the natural landscape, that it merely functions as a representative
of the animal kingdom. As he reads on, he will, of course, come to
recognize that the doe plays a central role, and yet he will not
necessarily realize that it is functioning as a symbol, for it might
well merely be an actual animal, though possibly one with magical
properties and powers. Even if our hypothetical reader begins to
lean towards a symbolic interpretation of the poem, he will not
find enough internal evidence to formulate a sensitive reading.
Does the deer represent a political figure, for example? Might it
represent some aspect of the speaker's own personality or life?
Questions like these seem absurd when we know the conventions
of Petrarch's genre, but if we attempt to read the sonnet while
deliberately forgetting these conventions, we see just how much
they normally influence our responses.

Gestalt psychologists are intrigued with the fact that we can
perceive certain visual phenomena, such as a pattern of black on
white tiles, in any number of different ways: certain tendencies
inherent in our brains, they assert, show us the right way of
'reading' the pattern. Their argument is also applicable to reading
in the more literal sense. As we have seen, one could interpret the
opening four lines of Petrarch's sonnet either as a description of a
deer that happens to be in a natural landscape or as a description of
a natural landscape that happens to include a deer; it is our generic
expectations that indicate which part of the pattern is most important and hence guide us to a just interpretation of Petrarch's
allegory. (Paul Hernadi explores parallels between genre and
Gestalt theory in *Beyond Genre*, pp. 5ff.)

But the process that the Gestalt psychologists analyze so well differs from the process of responding to a genre in certain crucial regards. First of all, those literary responses are not innate but learned ones. Moreover, according to some Gestalt theorists the perception of a visual pattern is an act that, once having occurred, excludes the simultaneous perception of an alternative pattern: at the moment when we regard the design as black on white, it is impossible for us also to regard it as white on black. In contrast, our responses to the genre or genres of a literary work constitute a complex series of visions and revisions. A writer may deliberately confound our tentative assumptions about the genre in which he is writing, or a work that is essentially in one literary form may include episodes in or allusions to many other literary forms as well. Above all, as we read we are often acutely conscious of the ways the writer is reshaping his genre even while working within it.

For codes may be violated, of course, and contracts broken. As we have seen, the reader brings to a literary work generic expectations shaped by previous encounters with other works in the same form. Often these assumptions are negative ones, whether about form or about content – a novel will not be written in verse, the lady in a sonnet will not be evil and so on. One of the most effective ways a writer can use genre is to evoke and intensify our generic expectations only to overturn them. The reader of *Sir Gawain and the Green Knight* learns no less than the hero because the violation of our expectations about romance shocks us into re-examining the values of the conventional romance, much as both Sir Gawain and the poet who created him are doing. Since Shakespeare's sonnets so signally refuse to play by the rules of their genre, we, like the speaker and the poet, become acutely conscious of those rules and, eventually, intensely suspicious of the attitudes to love implicit in the sonnet's conventions. In other words, it is by overturning our generic expectations that a writer can induce in his reader a series of intellectual reflections and emotional experiences very like those being enacted in and by the work itself.

*　　*　　*

Milton's 'Lycidas', a pastoral elegy on the death of his acquaint-
ance Edward King, exemplifies that process of reversing expectations perhaps better than any of the other works we have
examined so far. But this is only one of the ways Milton is reacting
to generic traditions; like so many of its author's other poems,
'Lycidas' testifies to the complexity and the intensity of his responses to his literary inheritance. *Pace* Dr Johnson, who severely
criticized the pastoral elegy in general and 'Lycidas' in particular,
the poem represents so skillful an interpretation of its literary form
that a reading of it at once encapsulates and extends many of the
points we have been exploring.

The very title announces a debt to other pastoral elegies and in
so doing prepares the reader to encounter other debts: both
Theocritus and Virgil assign the name 'Lycidas' to shepherds in
their own pastorals. Milton also borrows the general pattern of
classical pastoral elegies, a movement from lamentation to consol-
ation, and many of the topoi that customarily constitute that
structure. Here, as in Latin and Greek elegies, the speaker passion-
ately demands to know why those who might have saved the dead
man were not present when he perished. Like many of its classical
predecessors, the poem includes a list of human mourners. And
the pathetic fallacy, the attribution of human emotions to nature,
features no less prominently here than in those classical poems:
Milton declares that nature is mourning the dead man by dying
itself. The speaker's lamentation, like those in most Latin and
Greek pastoral elegies, culminates in the *consolatio* in which he
achieves and implicitly recommends to his readers a way of accepting the death.

Just as Milton borrows the Italian canzone for his stanza form
(and, as we shall see, also borrows certain theoretical assumptions
about the canzone), so he adapts several conventions from his
Italian predecessors. In particular, St Peter's famous denunciation
of corrupt clergymen

　　　And when they list, their lean and flashy songs

Grate on their scrannel pipes of wretched straw.
The hungry sheep look up, and are not fed

('Lycidas', 123–5)

grows out of a tradition established by Petrarch, Boccaccio and Mantuan of including satire, especially ecclesiastical satire, in pastorals.

As we have observed throughout this chapter, a concern for generic traditions, far from precluding originality, often helps to produce it. 'Lycidas' is no exception. Milton's original responses to the conventions of his genre extend across a broad spectrum, ranging from passages that merely apply generic conventions to a local situation or develop implications latent in other elegies to ones that reject the overt and central assumptions of such elegies. This spectrum reminds us again that, rather than occupying a simple and single position in relationship to other works in its genre (that is, the sort of position that conveniently lends itself to a label like 'unimaginative imitation' or 'parody'), a poem may as it progresses assume a whole series of different and even conflicting attitudes to its predecessors. It would be no less foolhardy to attempt to summarize in one phrase the attitudes to the pastoral elegy that are expressed or embedded in 'Lycidas' than it would be to attempt to encapsulate in a phrase the attitudes to death that we encounter in the poem.

Because both the poet and his subject were at Cambridge, the spirit of the river Cam figures among the mourners:

Next Camus, reverend sire, went footing slow,
His mantle hairy, and his bonnet sedge,
Inwrought with figures dim.

(103–5)

By choosing a river deity to personify the university, Milton links that god to all the other gods connected with water whom he invokes and, indeed, to an elaborate pattern of imagery about water. At the same time, by including Camus, Milton relates his mythic apparatus to King's actual life; functioning rather like Sidney's puns on the real name of Stella, Penelope Rich, this allusion to the Cam reminds us that the poet's pastoral fantasies reflect underlying biographical and psychological truths.

Milton's development of several inherited topoi are no less skillful than his evocation of Camus, and also no more threatening in their implications about his genre or generic traditions in general. In particular, as one reader points out, while several classical elegies do include a list of mourners, it is Milton himself who reshapes that list into the dramatic form of an actual procession (see J. B. Leishman, *Milton's Minor Poems*, pp. 256–73). And while a *consolatio* is the conventional culmination to an elegy, Milton's interpretation of that topos is decidedly unconventional in its amalgam of Christian and pagan responses to death: King achieves Christian rebirth through the intercession of 'him that walked the waves' (173), mythic rebirth through his new role as 'the genius of the shore' (183), a kind of symbolic rebirth through his participation in the diurnal cycle of the sun, and, of course, rebirth through the poem that celebrates him.

However, at the same time that the poem extends certain pastoral conventions it rejects many others. Milton's famous passage about poetic fame and human achievement in general

> Alas! What boots it with uncessant care
> To tend the homely slighted shepherd's trade,
> And strictly meditate the thankless Muse?
> Were it not better done as others use,
> To sport with Amaryllis in the shade

(64–8)

calls into question not only his own work as a poet but also one of the underlying assumptions of the pastoral elegy, the notion that poetry can and should immortalize. Rather than merely celebrating his art, as his predecessors in the pastoral elegy tend to do, he is criticizing it. We are all the more startled by and involved with the questions Milton is posing because they violate the generic expectations that have been so carefully established and confirmed elsewhere in the poem.

Similarly, in many pastoral elegies nature comes to symbolize rebirth and renewal. While not totally rejecting that view, Milton repeatedly draws attention to the fragility and the mutability of the natural world. The very flowers that he so lovingly evokes – 'Bring the rathe primrose that forsaken dies' (142) – are delicate spring blossoms, ones that, like King himself, may wither and die 'before the mellowing year' (5).

In many regards, then, Milton is reinterpreting the pastoral elegy in response to certain issues and certain sentiments not normally found in such poems. Behind these radical deviations from previous elegies may well lie a comprehensive redefinition of the form itself. In his recent *'Lycidas' and the Italian Critics* Clay Hunt argues that Milton is reshaping the pastoral elegy in accordance with certain theories promulgated by Italian critics: he is, as they recommended, using the canzone for weighty subjects, subjects normally associated with genres other than pastoral, and he is incorporating into his poem many elements generally seen as more characteristic of the tragic muse.

'Lycidas' demonstrates the danger, even the impossibility, of separating formal and generic considerations like the ones we have been examining from those old staples of literary criticism, 'theme' and 'content': throughout Milton's elegy genre functions not merely as the framework through which other preoccupations are considered but also as an overt preoccupation, a theme in its own right. That theme in turn refers back to a number of others in the poem. For Milton's explorations of genre both exemplify and actually enact many of the central issues, literary and non-literary, of 'Lycidas'.

First of all, the poem is, as some of its readers have observed, concerned with types of community or the violation of them. The speaker mourns the loss not only of Lycidas but also of the pastoral community in which the two of them participated when they frolicked 'Under the opening eyelids of the morn' (26), and he rejects the community he could share with a certain type of poet, those who indulge in courtly, witty verse. By adapting so ancient, so conventionalized a genre, however, he is assuming a role in another and more durable community, that of poets in his genre. The brief but poignant allusion to such writers early in the poem

> So may some gentle Muse
> With lucky words favour my destined urn,
> And as he passes turn,
> And bid fair peace be to my sable shroud

(19–22)

is very resonant and acquires added resonance as 'Lycidas' progresses: by the very act of writing his elegy, the speaker has taken his place in the tradition and hence, by continuing and contributing to it, he has encouraged his successors to perform for him a similar act of mourning.

Milton's speaker also enacts the central aesthetic issue in the poem, that of establishing a relationship to the values and the visions of pastoral. 'Lycidas' is, of course, deeply concerned with the functions of poesy, whether it be poesy as a languorous pastime or as an antidote to death or as a source of fame. The way the speaker shifts from one style to another, and even, according to Clay Hunt, in a sense from one genre to another, exemplifies the way we all must, as Milton implies, abandon the childhood joys of 'rural ditties' (32) or the satisfactions of courtly poetry for a graver response to experience – a response that both accepts and transcends pastoral, incorporating into it elements from other forms.

It is in the final lines that form mirrors content best and enacts this concern with pastoral most dramatically:

> Thus sang the uncouth swain to th' oaks and rills,
> While the still morn went out with sandals gray;
> He touched the tender stops of various quills,
> With eager thought warbling his Doric lay:

And now the sun had stretched out all the hills,
And now was dropped into the western bay;
At last he rose, and twitched his mantle blue:
Tomorrow to fresh woods, and pastures new.

(186–93)

Unlike many pastorals, this poem does not begin with a frame that introduces the speaker and hence sets him at a distance – why, then, does it end on one? The speaker of these final lines is separating himself from the poet-shepherd who delivered the rest of the poem, as he was unable or unwilling to do earlier; or, to put it another way, Milton is evolving a second speaker and one who is more removed from the pastoral world than the first. By setting the first speaker at a distance in this way, then, the poem and its poet are themselves acting out the very process 'Lycidas' has been analyzing, the process of stepping back from and evaluating the pastoral world and its participants. . . . Perhaps one is able to move on to pastures new only when and because one has defined one's relationship to older pastures, noting their limitations but also accepting one's links to them, as Milton's speaker has done in the course of the poem.

'Lycidas' demonstrates, then, how important it is for readers to compare a given work of art with other works in the same genre, to consider the ways our responses are and should be affected by our previous experiences with the literary form in question. 'Lycidas' demonstrates, too, how deep and how varied an author's responses to genre can be. In so doing it reminds us that Eliot's famous pronouncement about literary tradition is particularly applicable to the ways both writers and their readers respond to that important repository of literary tradition, genre:

> the historical sense compels a man to write not merely with his own generation in his bones, but with a feeling that the whole of the literature of Europe from Homer and within it the whole of the literature of his own country has a simultaneous existence and composes a simultaneous order. This historical sense,

which is a sense of the timeless as well as of the temporal and of the timeless and of the temporal together, is what makes a writer traditional. And it is at the same time what makes a writer most acutely conscious of his place in time, of his own contemporaneity.

No poet, no artist of any art, has his complete meaning alone. His significance, his appreciation is the appreciation of his relation to the dead poets and artists. You cannot value him alone; you must set him, for contrast and comparison, among the dead.

('Tradition and the individual talent', p. 4)

3
Genre theory I: Aristotle to Arnold

Such once were critics; such the happy few,
Athens and Rome in better ages knew.
The mighty Stagirite first left the shore,
Spred all his sails, and durst the deeps explore;

[. . .]

Poets, a race long unconfined and free,
Still fond and proud of savage liberty,
Received his laws; and stood convinced 'twas fit,
Who conquered Nature, should preside o'er Wit.
(Alexander Pope, *An Essay on Criticism*)

Many writers have observed that Shakespearean criticism provides
a useful touchstone to the underlying aesthetic attitudes of the
period that produces it. The same is true of genre theory. Concepts
of genre carry with them so many general implications about
literature that they regularly reflect in microcosm the poetics of
their author and of his age. If one knew nothing about a given writer
save his pronouncements on genre, one could predict many of his
other aesthetic principles, and predict them with great accuracy.

The very question of whether one should accept the notion of
generic classification or challenge its validity involves one of the
broadest theoretical issues, the degree of autonomy that can be
claimed for the work of art and its creator. That acceptance of
generic categories tends to imply – and also tends to encourage –
a view of the writer as a craftsman instructed by past artists, rather
than a bard inspired by his own emotions. The debate between
what might loosely be termed the neo-classical and the romantic
positions on this subject has been enacted both in the criticism of
the eighteenth and nineteenth centuries and in that of many other

ages as well. The way a critic chooses to describe and define genres – whether in terms of, say, their linguistic patterns or their underlying assumptions about time or their effects on the reader – reveals his presuppositions about the very nature of art. Indeed, genre criticism may embody responses not only to aesthetic problems but also to many social issues: concepts of generic evolution, for instance, often reflect attitudes about social and political change.

Despite the important differences among the theories propounded in different ages, certain recurrent preoccupations have characterized commentaries on genre in the more than two thousand years that separate Aristotle's *Poetics* from Frye's *Anatomy of Criticism*. One predictable concern has been the description and classification of genres: rhetoricians have debated the criteria by which literary forms should be defined, enumerated the characteristics of particular genres, traced the family resemblances between them and erected hierarchies based on the relative significance of these types. Such efforts at classification have proved especially complex and especially controversial in the case of the lyric, the epic and drama. Underlying all of these morphological considerations is the central problem that definitions of genres, like those of biological species, tend to be circular: one establishes such a definition on the basis of a few examples, and yet the choice of those examples from the multitude of possible ones implies a prior decision about the characteristics of the genre. The evolution of literary forms is another recurrent issue and one that has intrigued writers as diverse in all other ways as, for example, Sir Philip Sidney and Victor Hugo; among the principal questions are what factors, aesthetic or social or both, cause genres to change, and whether or not they reach a culmination, a point of perfection.

*   *   *

In Book III of Plato's *Republic*, Socrates asserts that there are three and only three methods of presenting a work of art: pure narration, in which the poet speaks in his own voice; 'narration by imitation', in which one or more speakers are bodied forth in the work; and a mixture of the two. Dithyrambic poetry, which was generally a form of ode in which the poet was accompanied instrumentally, is cited as an example of the first type; tragedy and comedy represent the second; the epic is an instance of the third or mixed form, as the poet intersperses dialogue in his own narration. The distinction between the three members of the triad that is established in Socrates' brief discussion was to appear – whether to be repeated, reinterpreted or reviled – in the writings of aestheticians during the following two thousand years.

It is, however, Aristotle's *Poetics* that represents the *locus classicus* of genre criticism; indeed, as Whitehead observed of philosophy after Plato, subsequent literary theory frequently reads like a series of footnotes to Aristotle. The opening words of the *Poetics* announce the central role that genre will assume in the pages that follow: 'I propose to treat of poetry in itself and of its various kinds, noting the essential quality of each' (p. 7). Aristotle proceeds to enumerate three principal methods of distinguishing those different species, methods that reflect his central assumption that art is an imitation (or, to use the alternative translation some scholars offer for *mimesis*, a representation) of nature. The first criterion is the medium in which they imitate reality – in other words, whether they use rhythm, melody, verse or some combination of these media. The second distinction is in what Aristotle terms the 'object of imitation':

> Since the objects of imitation are men in action, and these men must be either of a higher or a lower type (for moral character mainly answers to these divisions, goodness and badness being the distinguishing marks of moral differences), it follows that we must represent men either as better than in real life, or as worse, or as they are. . . . The same distinction marks off tragedy from comedy; for comedy aims at representing men as worse, tragedy as better than in actual life.

> (pp. 11, 13)

Brief though this statement may be, it has inspired the most lengthy addenda and refinements, including many by twentieth-century critics. Echoing the distinction postulated in *The Republic*, Aristotle proceeds to articulate a third difference between genres, the 'manner of imitation':

> For the medium being the same, and the objects the same, the poet may imitate by narration − in which case he can either take another personality as Homer does, or speak in his own person, unchanged − or he may present all his characters as living and moving before us.

> (p. 13)

The remainder of the treatise is largely devoted to enumerating the qualities of tragedy, comedy and epic. In so doing, Aristotle incorporates a whole range of criteria for defining and describing genres − the meters associated with them, their effect on the audience (here he develops his renowned theory that tragedy generates pity and fear) and their structure (for example both tragedy and epic must consist of a single action). Behind regulations like these lie certain presuppositions that were to prove no less influential than the rules they generate. Central to Aristotle's system is the concept of decorum: the notion that certain subjects require appropriate forms and styles. A tragic subject, for instance, demands a particular type of character and language. Aristotle's principles also carry with them an assumption that finds its clearest expression in his declaration that tragedy stopped developing when it had reached its natural form − that is, the characteristically classical belief that a perfect model does exist for each type of art, whether it be a temple or a tragedy. The role of the artist is not to express his individuality through exciting deviations from the art of the past, not to effect the process that Ezra Pound proudly labelled 'making it new', but rather to come as close as possible to that perfect and natural form. Many of the statements about genre issued by Aristotle's followers stem from their acceptance of this credo; and many of the statements issued by other critics reflect their desire to violate it, and to be seen to violate it.

Towards the end of the treatise Aristotle declares that tragedy is a higher form than epic: it enjoys all the advantages of epic and, in addition, proves more effective, since its compactness makes it more enjoyable and its immediacy renders it more vivid. This judgment, too, was to excite debate, with later aestheticians variously accepting Aristotle's ranking, placing epic in the ascendancy, or questioning the very notion that one genre can be superior to another.

What Aristotle does not say in the *Poetics*, however, has generated almost as much discussion as what he does. The brevity of his comments on lyric has puzzled many readers (some ascribe the absence of any sustained consideration of that mode to an unrealized intention to add another book to the *Poetics*, some to a reluctance to focus on a form whose relationship to his principle of imitation is tendentious). In any event, Aristotle's omission of such commentary has inspired a number of his followers throughout the centuries to enumerate for the lyric principles like those he himself establishes for dramatic and epic literature.

Immediately after the tribute to Aristotle, the 'mighty Stagirite', quoted at the beginning of this chapter, Horace is praised by Pope in very different terms:

> Horace still charms with graceful negligence,
> And without method talks us into sense,
> Will, like a friend, familiarly convey
> The truest notions in the easiest way.
>
> (*An Essay on Criticism*, 653–6)

As Pope's paean suggests, what is remarkable about Horace's verse epistle on aesthetics, the *Ars Poetica*, is not the originality of its ideas – much of this poem is in fact a distillation of other treatises – but rather the grace and good humor with which they are presented. The *Ars Poetica* was to prove highly influential. It was primarily through reading this work, rather than the *Poetics* itself, that many English writers became familiar with (though often misconceived) Aristotelian principles.

Adopting the Aristotelian precept that art should evince a unified and coherent structure, Horace's treatise opens:

> If a painter chose to join a human head to the neck of a horse, and to spread feathers of many a hue over limbs picked up now here now there, so that what at top is a lovely woman ends below in a black and ugly fish, could you, my friends, if favoured with a private view, refrain from laughing?
>
> (1–5)

Elsewhere, too, Horace lauds such Aristotelian values as unity and consistency. But as the epistle progresses the differences in manner that distinguish the Latin poet from his Greek predecessor also become increasingly apparent. Horace is far less concerned with theoretical questions about the nature of art and the nature of its effect on the audience, far more with pragmatic issues. He does not explore the 'deeps' of art, as Pope asserts that Aristotle does, but rather codifies unexceptional instructions for a smooth sailing on its lakes.

His commentary on genre is informed by his recurrent emphasis on decorum:

> no god, no hero, who shall be brought upon the stage, and whom we have just beheld in royal gold and purple, shall shift with vulgar speech into dingy hovels, or, while shunning the ground, catch at clouds and emptiness. Tragedy, scorning to babble trivial verses, will, like a matron bidden to dance on festal days, take her place in the saucy Satyrs' circle with some little shame.
>
> (227–33)

Metrical considerations predominate when Horace discusses genre, as they do in comparable discussions by many other classical writers:

> In what measure the exploits of kings and captains and the sorrows of war may be written, Homer has shown. . . . If I fail to keep and do not understand these well-marked shifts and shades

of poetic forms, why am I hailed as poet? . . . A theme for comedy refuses to be set forth in verses of tragedy.

(73–4, 86–7, 89)

Here, as throughout the treatise, its author's concern with craftsmanship is very apparent. Though the precepts he evolves for tragedy are similar to Aristotelian ones, Horace devotes far less space to that form, and to drama in general, than the author of the *Poetics* does; and he alludes to a number of literary types to which Aristotle had given little or no attention, such as elegies, hymns to gods, odes to athletes, love poetry and drinking songs.

The good sense and good humor that grace Horace's other epistles and satires are no less in evidence in the *Ars Poetica*. The writer who found the dialogue a peculiarly congenial form is here very willing to admit of exceptions to his rules; he notes, for example, that comedy does sometimes include a more elevated style than we would normally associate with it and tragedy a more lowly one.

The classical sources of English genre theory are not confined to treatises on poetics: such discussions of oratory as Quintilian's *Institutiones Oratoriae* also exercised an indirect but none the less powerful influence. It is likely that the practice of dividing types of literature into categories and establishing the rules for each received some impetus from the tradition of distinguishing epideictic (that is, concerned with praise or blame), judicial and deliberative oratory. It is also more than likely that many of the rules formulated for these oratorical types were applied by both classical and later theorists to the corresponding literary genres. Thus, for example, the convention that a speech praising a landscape should laud both its beauty and its utility found its way into the country-house poems of the seventeenth century. Moreover, the relationship between the norms of deliberative oratory and those of the verse epistle, a genre that at first glance seems notable for its relative absence of generic characteristics, deserves far more attention than it has received.

We are too prone to rest content with generalizations about the sources of English literature that are far more pat than the insights we offer about that literary tradition itself. Critics who read Sidney with exemplary subtlety will repeat the conventional wisdom about his Petrarchan models without embarrassment; those who comment intelligently on neo-classicism too often rely on clichés about classicism. We need to remind ourselves that the classical sources of genre theory do not always conveniently adhere to what we think of as classical principles. To be sure, Greek and Roman writers and theorists are very conscious of generic divisions; to be sure, they are very concerned with generic prescriptions. But even they accept some deviation from the regulations, an acceptance that provides an analogue to and quite possibly a source for the flexibility we find in many of their English successors. Quintilian, for example, advises us in the *Institutiones Oratoriae* that while we should imitate the models established by our predecessors, it is also important to invent new ways of writing. Comparing the slavish imitations he is condemning with the work of painters who copy other pictures with the aid of a ruler, he points out that if earlier writers had not seen fit to alter their models, art would still be at a very preliminary stage.

★   ★   ★

Despite their influence on Renaissance and later writers, Plato and Aristotle were hardly known in medieval England, while Cicero was studied primarily through a work now recognized as un-canonical, the *Rhetorica ad Herennium*. It was instead the Hellenistic rhetoricians who were the primary classical source for medieval critical theory. Admiring a florid style, many of these Greek aestheticians give far more space to enumerating rhetorical figures than to analyzing overall form and structure. They do, however, often list the three main kinds of poetry and spell out the decorum of each.

The comments on genre that are threaded through the work of the major medieval writers are generally brief and conventional.

Take, for example, *De Arte Metrica*, an aesthetic treatise by the Venerable Bede, the monk whose *Historia Ecclesiastica Gentis Anglorum* is one of the most important literary documents of the Anglo-Saxon period. Classical writers had considered prosody and genre so closely connected and genre so intrinsically significant that any discussion of metrics might well have devoted considerable attention to literary types. But Bede's tract does not. Briefly enumerating the three modes and listing a few instances of each, he analyzes genre only in one paragraph at the end of the treatise.

The distinction between tragedy and comedy appears with considerable regularity in the work of medieval writers and theorists, and Chaucer is no exception. In *The Canterbury Tales* the Monk repeats the customary generalizations about the subject; tragedy, he suggests, is a story

> Of hym that stood in great prosperitee,
> And is yfallen out of heigh degree
> Into myserie, and endeth wreccedly.
> ('Prologue', *The Monk's Tale*, 1975–7)

This definition helps to explain why Chaucer labels his *Troilus and Criseyde* a 'tragedye' (V, 1786).

Many medieval writers considered only the classical languages appropriate to serious art. Dante's *De Vulgari Eloquentia* is, as its title would suggest, a discussion – and a defense – of literature written in the 'vulgar' (in the sense of popular) Italian tongue. The decorum of several genres is spelled out, with especial attention to stylistic considerations. Tragedy, Dante writes, is a work in the high style, comedy in a lower one, and the elegy in the lowest; each of these forms has its fitting subject matter. To this traditional classification, however, he adds another distinction, the version of the vulgar tongue suited to each genre. Debating which variant of Italian is the purest and best, he rejects the claims proffered by various local dialects and instead praises a form of his language free from these local usages, which he terms *illustris* ('illustrious' or 'distinguished') Italian. It is this type that is appropriate to the highest literature, tragedy, while comedy may be written either in the 'illustrious' version of the language or a lower one. Dante also explores another ramification of decorum by suggesting that the canzone, the elaborate verse form that Milton adapts in 'Lycidas', is the best prosodic type available in Italian and hence befits the most worthy subjects.

The 'Letter to Can Grande', attributed by most modern scholars to Dante himself, repeats the familiar contrasts between the two principal types of drama – tragedy starts peacefully but ends horribly while comedy reverses the pattern, tragedy demands a lofty and comedy a humble style. It is on this basis, the author of the epistle maintains, that the title of Dante's *La Divina Commedia* may be understood and justified. Like earlier medieval treatises, the letter also includes a brief enumeration of other literary types, such as bucolic poetry, the elegy, satire and the hymn.

According to the conventional wisdom, the commentary on genre proffered by medieval rhetoricians is as perfunctory and as unoriginal as that of most medieval writers. If applied only to the early Middle Ages, that truism is in fact correct. Influenced by the Hellenistic rhetoricians and by their own emphasis on literature as a source of allegorically rendered spiritual verities rather than a construct of poetic devices, theorists of this period slight or totally ignore genre, as well as a number of the other formal considerations that were to intrigue their successors in the Renaissance. Save for brief summaries of the difference between tragedy and comedy or equally brief comments on the triad of dramatic, epic and lyric, they generally devote what little attention they do bestow on style to rhetorical devices. This relative indifference to literary form is reflected in the unembarrassed freedom with which the names of various genres were used; there were almost as many meanings assigned to the term 'romance', for example, as there were poets eager to work in that form.

The important recent research of A. J. Minnis, however, definitively undercuts much of the conventional wisdom about medieval poetics. He argues that in the thirteenth century many biblical scholars developed a serious and sustained interest in the literal sense of the Bible, an interest that generated what were essentially literary analyses of the Scriptures. Those analyses emphasize that the Bible encompasses many theological and stylistic modes. In studying the stylistic modes, which they label *formae tractandi* ('forms of treatment') or *modi agendi* ('modes of procedure'), these theologians enumerate a number of types that could be considered genres if that term is interpreted loosely – the prophetic books are said to contain the revelatory mode, the Psalms the oratorical mode and so on. Nor do these scholars merely rely on the work of their classical predecessors, as the customary generalizations about medieval poetics would lead us to predict: instead they proffer theories for a number of modes not included in the Greek and Latin rhetoric manuals, notably the prophetic. (For a more detailed exposition of these points, see the works by A. J. Minnis cited in the bibliography.)

*   *   *

The concise and apparently uncontroversial justification of the title *La Divina Commedia* in the 'Letter to Can Grande' stands in sharp and revealing contrast to the literary quarrels about genre in which so many of Dante's countrymen engaged during the Renaissance. Like Dante's poem, three Renaissance works, Ariosto's *Orlando Furioso*, Tasso's *Gerusalemme Liberata* and Guarini's *Il Pastor Fido*, all represent unconventional approaches to conventional genres; unlike Dante's poem, all excited battles as violent in their ways as the literal battles bodied forth by Ariosto and Tasso. The principal cause of dissension was that none of them fits neatly into the categories that Aristotle established: the first two are romances and as such violate many of the canons of the epic poetry that they superficially resemble, while the third is a tragicomedy. The aesthetic problems posed by such forms had been discussed in Italy previously; but the appearance of each of these works stimulated a more intense and more precisely focused debate.

The central issue, whether genres are fixed in their rules and limited in their number, crystallizes divergent attitudes to literary tradition in general and to Aristotle, the fount of so many literary traditions, in particular. In opposing new genres like romance, such Italian theorists as Antonio Sebastiano Minturno argue for the permanence and the immutability of literary types. The new genres are also condemned on the ground that they fit neither Aristotle's own categories nor his principle of determining genres by the object, manner and means of imitation. On the other hand, those rhetoricians who defend works like *Orlando Furioso* maintain that just as societies develop, so must their literary forms: Aristotle's rules cannot and should not be expected to apply without alteration to a world that has itself altered very much. But Aristotle's extraordinarily high repute is reflected in the fact that at certain points even the theorists who argue in favor of the new genres adduce the authority of the *Poetics* rather than challenging it. Defending his own tragicomedy, Guarini repeatedly refers to Aristotelian principles, maintaining, for example, that far from combining tragic, comic and pastoral plots, he is in fact presenting a single action.

The respect for Aristotle that so many Italian theorists manifested during this debate also characterizes their counterparts in the English Renaissance, who often start their treatises by paying homage to the author of the *Poetics* and quote him extensively thereafter. But it was still primarily through Horace's *Ars Poetica* that Aristotle's pronouncements were known. Horace's poem is frequently cited and not infrequently translated in full by English writers in the sixteenth and early seventeenth centuries; the Elizabethan rhetorician William Webbe, for example, appends a translation of the *Ars Poetica* to his treatise *A Discourse of English Poetry*, and Ben Jonson composes a version of it in rhymed couplets.

In the Renaissance, as in the Middle Ages, biblical scholarship provided yet another source (and yet another impetus) for genre studies. As Barbara Kiefer Lewalski has demonstrated, most extensively in her important recent study *Protestant Poetics and the Seventeenth-Century Religious Lyric*, the medieval idea that the

Bible encompasses most or even all literary forms is repeated and developed in Tudor and Stuart England. Writers of those periods cite Job as an instance of the epic, Psalm 45 as an example of the epithalamium and so forth; some claim that the Bible contains virtually all literary types, and George Wither, a minor seventeenth-century author, even goes so far as to assert that the principal modes may all be found within the Psalms.

Behind English debates on genre also lie the extensive continental discussions of the subject. The sixteenth-century rhetorician Julius Caesar Scaliger, whose *Poetices libri septem* is organized generically, proved especially influential; the fact that the Pléiade (a circle of French poets) tended to describe its proposed reforms of French poetry in terms of the genres that should variously be encouraged and abandoned may well have encouraged English poets to evaluate their own literary heritage, and their own contribution to it, generically.

Aristotle's pre-eminence helps to explain the repetition of many of his principles about genre, notably his stress on a unified structure, in Renaissance treatises. Classical criteria for describing literary forms are also regularly adduced: genres are often categorized in terms of the style in which they should be written and the social class that they concern, so that pastoral, for example, is typically described as a literary kind that evokes lowly shepherds and demands a suitably base style. The paradigm of Virgil's canon frequently informs such distinctions: as writers of the period are prone to point out, the *Georgics* exemplify the low style, the *Eclogues* the middle and the *Aeneid* the high.

Rhetoricians of the English Renaissance, however, often prove willing to deviate from classical genre theory. Though they readily accept that genres can and should be arranged in a hierarchy, Aristotle's own ranking of literary forms does not meet with universal approval: his claim that tragedy is the highest genre is accepted by some writers, but others, including so respected a figure as Sir Philip Sidney, assert that it is epic that deserves that title. Nor do theorists of the period consistently manifest the intense concern for meter that is so central in classical genre theory. While such essays as *Observations in the Art of English Poesy*, a treatise by the writer and musician Thomas Campion, do attempt to assign a specific meter to each literary form, others either touch on the issue more briefly or skirt it altogether. Many English rhetoricians implicitly abandon Aristotle's central credo of *mimesis* (or imitation) by discussing a range of literary forms, most notably history writing and lyric poetry, that do not readily fit within that definition of art.

The most striking point about genre theory during the English Renaissance, however, is not what is said but rather at what length and with what frequency it is said. Where genre is the subject of only a sketchy final paragraph in Bede's treatise, for example, it is an organizing principle and a primary preoccupation in many Renaissance discussions of poetics. One obvious explanation for the change from medieval attitudes is the increased interest in the example set by Aristotle and Horace, who devote so much attention to genre. Another is that writers of the English Renaissance were eager to establish the respectability of their own language. Like the French poets in the Pléiade, they equated a serious language with an elaborate system of rules and hence strove to demonstrate the respectability of their own vernacular tongue by finding or inventing quite as many rules as Greek and Latin could boast.

Rhetoricians of the English Renaissance are, then, no less concerned with genre than their neo-classical counterparts were to be. But they are far less strict about generic rules. Thus George Puttenham, the author of the influential volume *The Art of English Poesy*, briefly observes that romances violate some of the laws of epic, being in essence a different form, but he does not fault them on this or any other ground. For all his classicism, even Ben Jonson recommends a flexible approach to literary rules, including those pertaining to genres. As he declares in *Discoveries* when criticizing the Schoolmen, or scholastic philosophers, for their adulation of Aristotle:

Nothing is more ridiculous than to make an author a dictator, as the Schools have done with Aristotle. . . . For to many things a man should owe but a temporary belief and a suspension of his own judgement, not an absolute resignation of himself or a perpetual captivity. Let Aristotle and others have their dues; but if we can make further discoveries of truth and fitness than they, why are we envied?

(2095–103)

An attitude like the one Jonson expresses here is, of course, very much in evidence in the actual practice of writers, as Polonius' famous allusion to 'tragedy, comedy, history, pastoral, pastoral-comical, historical-pastoral, tragical-historical, tragical-comical-historical-pastoral' (*Hamlet*, II, ii, 403–6) reminds us. Even – or especially – Spenser's *Faerie Queene*, one of the greatest and most representative of sixteenth-century poems, juxtaposes elements of epic with those of that dubious form romance.

What lies behind this apparent inconsistency in the English Renaissance, this habit of on the one hand devising and defending generic norms while on the other casually, even cavalierly, accepting violations of them? To ascribe the paradox to the same flexibility that is present in attitudes to architectural form and manifest in the juxtaposition of, say, a classical portico with a mullioned window is tempting, but this answer begs the prior question of why such flexibility developed in the first place. The fact that the classical writers themselves condone some violation of the norms is suggestive. So, too, is the fact that much as the Bible was seen as a compendium of all genres, the *Iliad* and the *Odyssey* were viewed as containing in embryonic form a number of literary types. A writer who mixed genres could adduce ancient and honorable precedents.

One reason these and other precedents for deviating from generic norms proved so influential is that writers and rhetoricians in the English Renaissance apparently saw the process of writing in a genre not as the emulation of abstract and ideal models, as many of their classical and neo-classical counterparts did, but rather as the imitation of very specific ones. It is significant in this regard that the English Renaissance came on the heels of the Italian Renaissance: if English writers could not justify unconventional genres (or unconventional interpretations of traditional ones) by pointing to the canons of Aristotle, they could always refer instead to the actual achievements of, say, Ariosto or Guarini, or, alternatively, to those of earlier English writers.

Perhaps, too, the extraordinary social mobility in English Renaissance society encouraged and implicitly vindicated a concomitant sense of generic mobility. The financial and social position of the middle classes of course improved dramatically during the sixteenth century, a change signalled and spurred by Elizabeth's predilection for choosing her civil servants from that rank; in the next century, James I's rapid creation of new peers soon became notorious. Though the exact economic and social status of the aristocracy in Tudor and Stuart England is one of the most controversial issues in English historiography, there is no question but that at least some of its members were losing both the financial security and the political power that their forebears had taken for granted. Many of these changes involved not merely movement within the social hierarchy but also fundamental challenges to its principles, especially the notion that one's station in life is immutably determined by God himself. Such challenges were reflected in the frequency with which the sumptuary laws (regulations regarding the type of apparel permitted to each social group) were broken.

Certain links between literary and social systems had been firmly established long before the Renaissance: classical rhetoricians frequently expound the principle that tragedy concerns men of high estate and comedy characters of a lower class. Besides repeating those critical commonplaces, a number of Renaissance writers add more original applications of the parallel between literary and social classes; Jonson, for example, asserts in *Discoveries* that the epic demands more space than other forms, just as a king's house is naturally larger than a peasant's. Since writers were so conscious of the analogy between generic and social rankings, it seems more than possible that the social fluidity of the period encouraged and implicitly justified a flexible approach to genres.

Sidney's *An Apology for Poetry* is at once the greatest and the most typical aesthetic treatise of the English Renaissance. Like so many other Renaissance writers, Sidney seems to assume as a matter of course that much of his commentary should be organized along generic lines. Thus, for example, he defends art against its critics by enumerating the characteristics and the advantages of the principal genres:

> Is it then the pastoral poem which is misliked? For perchance where the hedge is lowest they will soonest leap over. Is the poor pipe disdained, which sometime out of Meliboeus' mouth can show the misery of people under hard lords or ravening soldiers? . . . Or is it the lamenting elegiac? . . . who surely is to be praised, either for compassionate accompanying just causes of lamentation, or for rightly painting out how weak be the passions of woefulness.
>
> (p. 116)

When evaluating generic norms, he evinces great respect for the relevant classical prescriptions but not an unthinking acceptance of them. The unities should be followed, he argues, not merely because Aristotle prescribed them but also because they make sense on their own terms: 'the stage should always represent but one place, and the uttermost time presupposed in it should be, both by Aristotle's precept and common reason, but one day' (p. 134). Like several of his contemporaries, he takes issue with Aristotle's ranking of the genres:

> But if anything be already said in the defence of sweet poetry, all concurreth to the maintaining the heroical, which is not only a kind, but the best and most accomplished kind of poetry. For as

the image of each action stirreth and instructeth the mind, so the lofty image of such worthies most inflameth the mind with desire to be worthy, and informs with counsel how to be worthy.

(p. 119)

Sidney's opposition to mixed genres, though unmistakable, in fact seems to be more tempered and more temperate than we usually acknowledge. 'But besides these gross absurdities', he writes, 'how all their plays be neither right tragedies, nor right comedies, mingling kings and clowns, not because the matter so carrieth it, but thrust in clowns by heads and shoulders, to play a part in majestical matters, with neither decency nor discretion' (p. 135). Here, as in the statement on the unities that I quoted earlier, he is asserting that common sense, not an automatically adopted tradition, should be our guide. It is suggestive, too, that while in this case (and presumably in the majority of others) the dictates of good sense coincide conveniently with those of Aristotle, Sidney's criterion of judgment leaves open the possibility that at times they may not coincide, at times the matter may even 'carry' that mingling of kings and clowns.

The dovetailing of different intellectual traditions that is one of the characteristics and one of the achievements of Christian humanism finds full expression in the statements on genre with which so many of Milton's essays are studded: the classical rhetoricians are perhaps the principal source of these observations, but Milton supplements their precepts with the arguments of Renaissance theorists, the practice of patristic writers and the evidence of the Bible itself. In 'Of Education' (*The Complete Prose Works of John Milton*) he advocates learning the rules for epic, dramatic and lyric poetry, naming as authorities not only Aristotle and Horace but the Italian commentators as well; similarly, the preface to *Samson Agonistes*, which is in effect a brief essay on tragedy, cites as models both the great Greek tragedians and one of the Church Fathers. Biblical examples feature prominently in the discussion of genres incorporated into 'The Reason of Church-Government' (*Complete Poetry and Major Prose*); Milton describes the Song of Solomon, for example, as 'a divine pastoral drama' and calls the Apocalypse of St John 'a high and stately tragedy' (p. 815).

That same essay testifies that his theories about genre guided Milton during a crucial decision in his own poetic development. He explains that he developed the ambition to 'leave something so written to aftertimes, as they should not willingly let it die' (p. 810). In pursuit of that ambition, he reports, he scrutinized a wide range of precedents, debating the relative merits of tragedy and epic and evaluating the generic norms customarily associated with each of them:

> whether that epic form whereof the two poems of Homer, and those other two of Virgil and Tasso are a diffuse, and the Book of Job a brief model: or whether the rules of Aristotle herein are strictly to be kept, or nature to be followed, which in them that know art, and use judgement is no transgression, but an enriching of art. (p. 813)

*   *   *

The very titles of neo-classical critical essays – Dryden's 'An Essay of Dramatic Poesy', Farquhar's 'A Discourse upon Comedy', Rymer's 'A Short View of Tragedy', Goldsmith's 'An Essay on the Theatre; or, A Comparison between Sentimental and Laughing Comedy' and so forth – testify to an extraordinary preoccupation with genre. The subject also figures prominently, of course, even in many treatises whose titles do not so obviously signal an interest in it; Boileau devotes much of the second canto of his *L'art poétique*, a poem highly influential in England as well as on the continent, to enumerating the genres and their rules, while Pope's *An Essay on Criticism* is packed with allusions to literary forms.

One of the most exploratory approaches to genre during the neo-classical period is Thomas Hobbes's reply to William Davenant's preface to his epic poem *Gondibert*. Each genre, Hobbes argues, is associated with a particular geographical region:

> As philosophers have divided the universe, their subject, into three regions, celestial, aerial, and terrestrial, so the poets . . . have lodged themselves in the three regions of mankind, court, city, and country, correspondent in some proportion to those three regions of the world.
>
> (p. 55)

Hobbes's schematic enumeration serves to remind us that the neo-classical belief that the genres form an ordered hierarchy reflects attitudes not only to social systems but also to cosmological ones: in fact, it is no accident that the era that delighted in producing orreries (models of the universe that showed the relative positions and the movements of the planets) also took pleasure in systematizing the genres by spelling out their ranks and their interrelationships.

Linking each of the regions he specifies with a narrative or dramatic 'manner of representation', Hobbes proceeds to argue that there are and can be only six types of poetry: heroic dramatic (tragedy), heroic narrative (epic), scommatique (or 'scoffing') dramatic (comedy), scommatique narrative (satire), pastoral dramatic (pastoral comedy) and pastoral narrative (pastoral bucolic). The obvious objection, that this system omits such forms as the sonnet and the epigram, is countered with the strained rejoinder that those forms are not poems in their own right but rather essays or parts of poems. Whatever the limitations of Hobbes's analysis of the genres, it is interesting in its attempt to provide a systematic account of genre and also in its effort, more characteristic of later ages than Hobbes's own, to study genres in terms not of the rules they require but rather the temperaments they express.

John Dryden's critical writings, highly respected in Restoration and Augustan England, exemplify both the extent and the nature of the neo-classical interest in genre. Dryden repeatedly describes and evaluates literature in terms of its form, either carefully articulating the rules appropriate to a literary type or measuring a particular work against the relevant norms. Thus in 'An Essay of Dramatic Poesy' Neander, the character in the dialogue who represents Dryden, opens his examination of Jonson's *The Silent Woman* by noting that it observes the unities of time, place and action and hence accords to one of the central laws of its genre:

> To begin first with the length of the action, it is so far from exceeding the compass of a natural day, that it takes not up an artificial one. 'Tis all included in the limits of three hours and a half, which is no more than is required for presentment on the stage. A beauty perhaps not much observed. . . . The scene of it is laid in London; the latitude of place is almost as little as you can imagine, for it lies all within the compass of two houses, and after the first act, in one. The continuity of scenes is observed more than in any of our plays, except his own *Fox* and *Alchemist*.
> (pp. 58–9)

Another early essay, the preface to his poem 'Annus Mirabilis', also testifies to his concern for generic laws: he is careful here to distinguish this poem from epic, asserting that since it lacks a single action it should instead be termed a 'historical' work. Arguing that diction is in fact a less significant characteristic of epic than the overall design, in the 'Preface to the Fables' Dryden takes issue with Hobbes's theories about that genre. The dedication to the *Aeneis* includes another and equally conventional analysis of epic: here Dryden again upholds the Aristotelian dictum that the action of an epic must be single, entire and great and also emphasizes that such poems should be characterized by a consistently grave tone, a requirement that Ariosto fails to meet.

In the essay Dryden composed in defense of 'An Essay of Dramatic Poesy' we find perhaps the fullest explanation for this recurrent preoccupation with generic laws. Like Sidney and Milton, Dryden asserts that such rules are ultimately based on nature itself – or, as Pope was to put it in his *An Essay on Criticism*,

'Those rules of old discovered, not devised, / Are Nature still, but Nature methodized' (88–9). Dryden goes on to argue that the authority of Aristotle and Horace, as well as the more recent precepts and examples of Jonson and Corneille, lend further weight to generic norms. His allusion to Corneille, like many other passages in neo-classical criticism, reminds us of how conscious English writers were of the example set by the stringent French neo-classical critics and writers. There is often more than a trace of competitiveness, of, as it were, keeping up with the Boileaus, in literary theory.

Despite his evident respect for literary laws, Dryden accepts and even welcomes certain deviations from Aristotelian axioms. In several essays, for example, he takes issue with Aristotle's elevation of epic over tragedy. Though he does praise the French for observing the decorum of comedy better than his own countrymen, he faults them for a 'servile' adherence to literary laws and recommends a more capacious interpretation of such dicta:

> I acknowledge that the French contrive their plots more regularly, and observe the laws of comedy, and decorum of the stage (to speak generally), with more exactness than the English . . . yet, after all, I am of opinion that neither our faults nor their virtues are considerable enough to place them above us.
>
> For the lively imitation of nature being in the definition of a play, those which best fulfil that law ought to be esteemed superior to the others. 'Tis true, those beauties of the French poesy are such as will raise perfection higher where it is, but are not sufficient to give it where it is not: they are indeed the beauties of a statue, but not of a man.
>
> ('An Essay of Dramatic Poesy', p. 44)

Like Dryden, Pope evinces both a respect for the rules and a recognition that they are not the sole determinant of good poetry:

> Learn hence for ancient rules a just esteem;
> To copy nature is to copy them.

Some beauties yet no precepts can declare,
For there's a happiness as well as care.
Music resembles poetry, in each
Are nameless graces which no methods teach,
And which a master hand alone can reach.
If, where the rules not far enough extend,
(Since rules were made but to promote their end)
Some lucky licence answer to the full
Th' intent proposed, that licence is a rule.

(*An Essay on Criticism*, 139–49)

The terms in which he defends decorum – 'For different styles
with different subjects sort / As several garbs with country, town,
and court' (322–3) – hint again that in the minds of many writers
the idea of an orderly poetic system was linked, however subter-
raneanly, with that of an orderly social system. Hence weaving dis-
cordant elements into the texture of a genre could be seen as
accepting and perhaps even inviting similar irregularities in the
social fabric.

Though published in 1759, Edward Young's *Conjectures on
Original Composition* does not echo the respect for literary rules
expressed by Pope and so many other neo-classical writers; in this
and several other respects, the essay instead anticipates some of the
canons of romantic critics. Young, adapting the concept of genius
developed by the classical writer Longinus, distinguishes inferior,
imitative works of art from what he terms 'originals':

Originals are, and ought to be, great favourites, for they are great
benefactors; they extend the republic of letters, and add a new
province to its dominion. Imitators give us only a sort of
duplicates of what we had. . . . All eminence and distinction lies
out of the beaten road; excursion and deviation are necessary to
find it; and the more remote your path from the highway, the
more reputable . . . rules, like crutches, are a needful aid to the
lame, though an impediment to the strong.

(pp. 6–7, 11–12, 14)

Literary rules, then, violate nature rather than reflecting it, and literary models of all types, including the generic, are not a pre-requisite for but rather an impediment to significant artistic achievement.

One of the most influential critical works of the neo-classical era is Hugh Blair's *Lectures on Rhetoric and Belles Lettres*, a compilation of lectures he delivered when Regius Professor at Edinburgh. The book enjoyed a great vogue, evidently enhanced by the respectability and the popularity its author had achieved as a clergyman; in fact, it has gone through some 130 editions since its original publication in 1783. Blair includes many conventional expositions of Aristotelian dicta, asserting, for example, that epic must consist of only one action. But elsewhere he defends works that other critics had faulted for what he considers inconsequential deviations from Aristotelian norms. He takes issue with another defender of generic conventions, the dogmatic neo-classical critic René Le Bossu; though Dryden had lauded that Frenchman as the greatest living critic, Blair maintains that he distorts the nature of literature by considering the epic poet a philosopher composing a treatise on morality rather than a creative artist.

Not the least of the attractions of Blair's *Lectures on Rhetoric and Belles Lettres* is in a sense a tangential one: they are interesting for what they imply about the origins of genre criticism as well as for what they contribute to it. Blair suggests that far from attaining a peak in contemporary literature, as Aristotle claimed tragedy had done in his time, certain forms may actually have declined:

> Poetry, however, in its ancient original condition, was perhaps more vigorous than it is in its modern state. It included then, the whole burst of the human mind; the whole exertion of its imaginative faculties. . . . The early bard . . . sung indeed in wild and disorderly strains; but they were native effusions of his heart; they were the ardent conceptions of admiration or resentment, of sorrow or friendship, which he poured forth. It is no wonder, therefore, that in the rude and artless strain of the first

poetry of all nations, we should often find somewhat that captivates and transports the mind.

(II, 322–3)

Similar sentiments, often expressed in strikingly similar language, recur in many nineteenth- and twentieth-century statements on genre, and they may lead us to ponder on the ways emotional responses, as well as more detached intellectual judgments, may shape our discussions of that subject. Many writers in effect turn analyses of literary forms into speculations on the differences between their own society and the societies that generated literary types that seem more fruitful or less 'decadent'. Such speculations are perhaps prompted in part by an urge to lament the in-adequacies of one's own culture while celebrating the dream of a Golden Age, a world elsewhere, and they are sometimes expressed with a wistfulness curiously reminiscent of the mood that finds fuller and franker realization in certain types of pastoral poetry.

Many neo-classical essays focus on the characteristics of a particular genre rather than a particular artist or poem. Addressing the intriguing problem of how a literary type that evokes so much pain can in fact bring pleasure to its viewers, David Hume's 'Of Tragedy' argues that such pleasure derives from admiring the writer's eloquence as well as from witnessing an imitation of life. In other critical essays, the writer weighs a given poem against the norms of its genre, as Joseph Addison does in the *Spectator* columns that examine the extent to which *Paradise Lost* conforms to the rules for an epic.

As is so often the case in critical theory, what neo-classical critics do not do is quite as revealing as what they do. Hobbes provides an interesting exception to the rule, but by and large his con-temporaries indulge in neither the kinds of abstract hypotheses about the origins of genre that had enjoyed a vogue in the Renaissance nor the speculations about its nature that were to become popular in the early nineteenth century; as Austin Warren and René Wellek suggest, this may well be because the writers in question take genre so completely for granted (*Theory of Literature*, p. 239). Nor do they theorize much about the artistic temperaments and the societal patterns that are likely to produce one literary form rather than another; that question, too, was to prove as congenial to romantic critics as it was foreign to their neo-classical predecessors. What does engage them above all, as we have seen, is repeating and refining the rules for each genre and testing particular works against those norms. They also return frequently to the problem of the hierarchy of genres, sometimes accepting and sometimes challenging Aristotle's pronouncement about the supremacy of tragedy.

A modern reader may be tempted to posit a neat dichotomy between the Renaissance flexibility about genre and neo-classical rigidity, tempted to stress how readily and how frequently the fascination with generic norms that we have been examining degenerated into a mechanistic application of them. Certainly we can often fault the minor critics of the period, and occasionally fault the major ones as well, in these terms. But the best neo-classical writers in fact remind us that the very rules they are so eager to invoke must admit of appeals to two higher courts, nature and common sense. Rebutting the purist objections to tragi-comedy, Samuel Johnson declares in his *Preface to Shakespeare*:

> Shakespeare has united the powers of exciting laughter and sorrow not only in one mind, but in one composition. . . . That this is a practice contrary to the rules of criticism will be readily allowed; but there is always an appeal open from criticism to nature. The end of writing is to instruct; the end of poetry is to instruct by pleasing. That the mingled drama may convey all the instruction of tragedy and comedy cannot be denied, because it includes both in its alternations of exhibition, and approaches nearer than either to the appearance of life, by showing how great machinations and slender designs may promote or obviate one another.
>
> (p. 67)

But why is it that genre interests the critics and the writers of this era so deeply? The most obvious response – their respect for the classics led them to adopt the classical preoccupation with genre – may also be the most important one. In addition, the neo-classical concern for generic forms no doubt was encouraged by, and in turn encouraged, the coexisting predilection for other types of carefully regulated forms, whether they be literary ones like the couplet or architectural ones like Palladian buildings. One of the most recurrent metaphors for art in this period is in fact architecture.

Such critics as Maynard Mack and W. C. B. Watkins have maintained that the Age of Reason had its roots in an intense consciousness of our propensity to be unreasonable, that the blessed rage for order that characterizes this period stems from a profound fear of disorder in the individual psyche and in the body politic. Attitudes to genre often mirror perceptions about other types of literary and extra-literary experience, and this issue is probably no exception: one explanation for the neo-classical preoccupation with generic norms is a sense of how deeply they were needed. Pope writes,

> Nature to all things fixed the limits fit,
> And wisely curbed proud man's pretending wit.
> As on the land while here the ocean gains,
> In other parts it leaves wide sandy plains.
>
> (*An Essay on Criticism*, 52–5)

While the ostensible purpose of this image is to testify to the potency of nature's curbs, it is suggestive that 'proud man's pretending wit' is like an ocean, a force that is potentially very violent and potentially very hard indeed to control.

* * *

In the difference between the neo-classical statements on genre and their analogues in romantic criticism we encounter in microcosm the broader distinctions between those two schools.

Where neo-classical critics respect generic rules, their counterparts in the next era typically reject those norms and at times even the whole concept of genre. Behind this contrast, of course, lies the romantic interest in the individual, the idiosyncratic, whether it be a personality or a work of art. Samuel Johnson advises us in *Rasselas* not to number the streaks of the tulip, not to lose ourselves in the individualized details at the expense of observing the overall form of the flower; the romantics, in contrast, delight in the shadings of those streaks. When English romantic critics do write about genre, they bring to it a preoccupation related to the biographical orientation that characterizes their approach to individual works of art: they explore the ways the form in question was shaped by the spirit of its age and the temperament of its author. Such critics study not the strictures but the spirit of genre, not their physiology but their psychology.

Similar theoretical questions inform the discussions of genre that feature so prominently in German philosophy and literary criticism during the romantic era. Hegel, one of the most influential of the German idealists (a school that stresses the importance of mind rather than any external physical reality), writes on genre at length in his *Aesthetik*. There he focuses particularly on describing and comparing the three members of the triad, lyric, epic and dramatic. One of the issues he explores is the type of society that produces each of those modes; epic, for example, reflects 'the child-like consciousness of a people [who feel] no separation between freedom and will' (II, 1045). In lyric events stem from a subjective mood, in drama from individuality of character, while in epic character and external circumstances are equally important. Some of Hegel's comparisons are predictable, but many of them overturn the conventional wisdom about the genres; he suggests, for instance, that fate is in fact more powerful in epic than in drama, for in the latter the character shapes his own fate.

Hegel's philosophical system is, of course, informed by his theory of dialectical movement, and it is on that principle that his comparisons between the genres culminate. He finds in the relationship between the three modes a dialectical pattern in which the thesis of lyric and the antithesis of epic issue in the synthesis of drama:

> The third and last mode of presentation conjoins the two previous ones into a new whole in which we see in front of us both an objective development and also its origin in the hearts of individuals. . . . Thus here, as in epic, an action is spread out before us with its conflict and the issue of it; . . . But the action is not presented to our vision in the purely external form of something that has really happened, i.e. as a past event brought to life by mere narrative; on the contrary, we see it actually present, issuing from the private will, from the morality or immorality, of the individual characters, who thus become the centre as they are in the principle of lyric.
>
> (II, 1038)

Goethe, like many other romantic writers, also explores the triad. In 'Uber epische und dramatische Dichtung', an essay he composed in collaboration with Schiller, literary modes are related to temporal ones, an idea that we shall encounter frequently in nineteenth- and twentieth-century genre theory. The epic poet, Goethe and Schiller suggest, narrates an event as completely past, while the dramatist presents it as completely present. They proceed to juxtapose two figures, the rhapsodist and the actor, and to compare the modes they represent: the rhapsodist or lyric poet does not appear in his poem while the actor is obviously present, the rhapsodist induces calm while the actor stimulates the audience's senses, the rhapsodist appeals to his listeners' imagination while the actor demands that we suppress our imagination when following the events on stage. Goethe explores genre elsewhere as well; within *Wilhelm Meisters Lehrjahre*, for example, may be found a comparison of the novel and drama.

Another continental analogue to English genre theory during the romantic period is the work of Victor Hugo. Reacting against the neo-classical reliance on rules and the cold, artificial literature that he believed it generated, he declares in the 1826 preface to his *Odes et Ballades*:

> On the subject of literary productions, one hears talk every day of the 'dignity' of such a genre, the 'appropriateness' of another . . . 'tragedy' forbids what the novel 'permits'. . . . The writer of this book has the bad fortune not to understand all that at all.
>
> (p. 7)

Like the neo-classical critics whom he is condemning, Hugo asserts that nature should be our ultimate guide when we write – but he of course sees nature not as the origin of literary rules but rather as an alternative to them. Indeed, the dialogue on genre between neo-classical writers like Le Bossu and their romantic successors such as Hugo crystallizes the different responses to nature – in the many senses of that term – that distinguish those two schools. Hugo's assumptions on the subject become explicit later in the preface when he compares works composed according to neo-classical rules with the artificial regularity of the royal gardens at Versailles and ones written without those restrictions to the more pleasing beauty of a New World landscape (a dichotomy with political undertones as well as more overt aesthetic implications). At the end of the preface Hugo offers an alternative to the neo-classical preoccupation with genre: 'The poet ought to have no more than one model, nature; no more than one guide, the truth. He should not write with that which has been written before but with his soul and with his heart' (p. 8). When Hugo does scrutinize generic types, as he does in the lengthy preface to his play *Cromwell*, his method is to associate the ages of history with their characteristic forms. In addition to relating genres to the life cycles of societies, he links them to the life cycles of individuals, arguing that lyric corresponds to birth, epic to action and drama to death.

The same distrust of genre expressed by Hugo had already been suggested both implicitly and explicitly throughout Wordsworth's preface to the *Lyrical Ballads*. This essay declares its distance from conventional neo-classicism as much by what it leaves out as by what it includes, and the absence of a sustained discussion of genre is especially telling: though Wordsworth comments at length on any number of other literary problems, he devotes only the briefest attention to literary forms. When he does touch on the subject, he does so to express doubts about its significance:

> The proper manner of treating trivial and simple verses . . . is not to say, this is a bad kind of poetry, or, this is not poetry, but, this wants sense. . . . Why trouble yourself about the species until you have previously decided the genus? Why take pains to prove that an ape is not Newton, when it is self-evident that he is not a man?
>
> (p. 155)

Coleridge's approach to genre is more complex and less consistent than that of Wordsworth. At times he seems to dismiss the subject as firmly as the author of the *Lyrical Ballads* does:

> We call, for we see and feel, the swan and the dove both transcendently beautiful. As absurd as it would be to institute a comparison between their separate claims to beauty from any abstract rule common to both, without reference to the life and being of the animals themselves – say rather if, having first seen the dove, we abstracted its outlines, gave them a false generalization, called them principle or ideal of bird-beauty and then proceeded to criticise the swan or the eagle – not less absurd is it to pass judgement on the works of a poet on the mere ground that they have been called by the same class-name with the works of other poets of other times and circumstances, or any ground indeed save that of their inappropriateness to their own end and being, their want of significance, as symbol and physiognomy.
>
> (*Shakespearean Criticism*, I, 196)

Later in the same group of notes, however, he suggests that genre can serve certain useful functions; in a passage reminiscent of similar statements by both Dr Johnson and Schlegel, he asserts that rather than dismissing all generic considerations from our reading of Shakespeare, we should refine and expand the categories:

> If the tragedies of Sophocles are in the strict sense of the word tragedies, and the comedies of Aristophanes comedies, we must emancipate ourselves of a false association from misapplied names, and find a new word for the plays of Shakespeare. They are in the ancient sense neither tragedies nor comedies, nor both in one, but a different genus, diverse in kind, not merely different in degree, – romantic dramas, or dramatic romances.
>
> (I, 197)

Elsewhere he adopts a more conventional position, asserting that we should not only accept generic classifications and the hierarchy of genres but also use these criteria to guide our critical judgments. Of *Paradise Lost* he writes: 'In its kind it is the most perfect poem extant, though its kind may be inferior in interest – being in its essence didactic – to that other sort, in which instruction is conveyed more effectively, because less directly' (*Miscellaneous Criticism*, p. 166). Though these conflicts in Coleridge's thought evidently reflect some personal confusions and inconsistencies, they also serve to remind us once again of the danger of accepting familiar labels like 'neo-classical' or 'romantic' without qualification, of oversimplifying literary history by forgetting that it often assumes the pattern of a continuum rather than that of a dialectical opposition.

Coleridge's reading in German philosophy is especially apparent in his discussions of the triad. He repeats the familiar distinction between the subjectivity of lyric and the objectivity of epic and proceeds to explore other aspects of the three modes:

> The first form of poetry is the epic, the essence of which may be stated as the successive in events and characters . . . in the epic, as in the so-called poems of Homer, the whole is completely

objective, and the representation is a pure reflection. The next form into which poetry passed was the dramatic; – both forms have a common basis with a certain difference, and that difference not consisting in the dialogue alone. Both are founded on the relation of providence to the human will; and this relation is the universal element, expressed under different points of view according to the difference of religions, and the moral and intellectual cultivation of different nations. In the epic poem fate is represented as overruling the will, and making it instrumental to the accomplishment of its designs. . . . In the drama, the will is exhibited as struggling with fate, a great and beautiful instance and illustration of which is the Prometheus of Aeschylus.

(*Shakespearean Criticism*, I, 138)

*   *   *

Nothing illustrates the interpenetration of aesthetic and cultural factors better than genre theory during the Victorian period. On one level that theory represents a self-conscious rejection of the romantic emphasis on the artist's autonomy and hence participates in the kind of debate between one age and the next that so often informs literary culture. On another level, Victorian attitudes to genre stem from the scientific and social milieu of their own age and reflect in particular the extraordinary impact of Darwinism.

John Addington Symonds' essay 'On the application of evolutionary principles to art and literature' exemplifies this interpenetration of the literary and the extra-literary. Darwin may have been slow to recognize the broader implications of his principles, but his contemporaries were not: Symonds, like so many other Victorian writers, reshapes the issue of generic evolution by approaching it through Darwin's discoveries. Hence he focuses not on the ideal form a particular literary type may achieve but rather on the movement from one type to another, on what his contemporary George Meredith describes as 'Change, the strongest son of Life' ('The Woods of Westermain', 258). Anthropomorphizing the evolutionary process in question, Symonds presents the familiar argument that the pattern followed by the arts corresponds to the three stages of human life, infancy, maturity and decline. It is this pattern, he maintains, not the temperament of the individual artist, that determines generic evolution. His grimly expressed emphasis on the writer's inability to surmount the stage at which his society finds itself may well remind us of the many Victorian novels in which characters are entrapped by their social milieu.

In *Shakspere's Predecessors in the English Drama* Symonds practices the sort of criticism he preaches in the essay we have examined. Stressing the biological metaphor, he repeats the argument that the arts describe an evolutionary pattern and proceeds to read English drama in light of that movement:

> Three stages may be marked in the short but vigorous evolution of our dramatic literature. The first and longest is the stage of preparation and of tentative endeavour. In the second maturity is reached. . . . The third is a stage of decadence and dissipation; the type, brought previously to perfection, suffers from attempts to vary or refine upon it. . . . The style of England, the expression of our race in a specific form of art, grew steadily, instinctively, spontaneously, by evolution from within. . . . Over the second period Shakspere reigns paramount. . . . We . . . who regard the evolution of the drama from the vantage-ground of time, see that in Shakspere the art of sixteenth-century England was completed and accomplished.
>
> (pp. 2–5)

Darwin's effect on literary theory, like his influence on scientific thought, was, of course, hardly confined to his own country: many continental writers also adopted evolutionary language and the concepts behind it when analyzing the origins of literary species. One of the most thorough applications of Darwinian theories is that of Ferdinand Brunetière, whose *L'évolution des genres dans l'histoire de la littérature* relates literary evolution to social changes, linking the development of satire, for example, to the rise of a 'bourgeois spirit' and a greater sense of independence and individualism. Though Brunetière does not develop his points systematically, he does raise some provocative ideas about the ways literary forms develop from each other and in so doing anticipates the more subtle arguments of the Russian formalists on the same subject:

> the differentiation of genres works in history like that of the species in nature, progressively, by transition from the single to the multiple, from the simple to the complex, from the homogeneous to the heterogeneous.
>
> (I, 20)

> each of these successive forms . . . appeared to us, at its beginnings, as a dismemberment and, during its development, as an extension of the preceding one.
>
> (I, 5)

If Symonds' statements on genre are the most representative Victorian criticism on the subject, Matthew Arnold's are the most impressive: he approaches the central issues about literary types with his customary blend of sensitivity and good sense. On the subject of generic rules his work displays a considerable debt to Aristotle. The preface to *Merope* quotes the author of the *Poetics* with evident approval, and the discussions of epic in the 1853 Preface repeat Aristotelian principles, as well as reflecting an Aristotelian concern for the overall structure of a work. That essay also includes a suggestive hint about one of the more subterranean reasons for his allegiance to the rules:

> But I say, that in the sincere endeavour to learn and practise, amid the bewildering confusion of our times, what is sound and true in poetical art, I seemed to myself to find the only sure guidance, the only solid footing, among the ancients. They, at any rate, knew what they wanted in art, and we do not. It is this uncertainty that is disheartening, and not hostile criticism.
>
> (p. 14)

Arnold was deeply troubled by the signs of chaos, social and literary, that he saw all around him, by the cacophony of ignorant armies clashing by night. The passage just cited hints that he may have seen in literary forms something similar to what I have suggested some of the neo-classical critics saw, a counterbalance to the types of turmoil that distressed him so deeply.

Several other essays amplify his respect for generic conventions; like so many other critics before him, Arnold suggests that these rules should be respected not because they have been established by authorities and hallowed by previous writers but rather because they make good sense. In 'On translating Homer', for example, he supports his contention that the ballad is naturally inappropriate for weighty subject matter by juxtaposing a poem that Wordsworth chose to cast in the ballad form with a more solemn one to which that poet rightly assigned a different meter.

But if Arnold respects generic rules, he also recognizes the need to alter them. In the preface to *Merope*, for instance, he asserts that the norms of Greek tragedy are not necessarily the best ones. As Coleridge before him had done, Arnold argues that Greek tragedy assumed the form it did in part because of the physical conditions of the Greek theater. In another age, he maintains, it could and should assume different forms: 'Travelling in a certain path, the spirit of man arrived at Greek tragedy; travelling in other paths, it may arrive at other kinds of tragedy' (p. 58).

Like Symonds and many other nineteenth-century writers, Arnold is concerned to link genres to particular stages of society. The ballad, he suggests, is associated with a simple and not very reflective period in human history. But, unlike many of his contemporaries, he refuses to employ this sort of observation in order to establish a hierarchy of genres. Anticipating the vehement rejections of such hierarchies by many modern critics, Arnold declares in 'On translating Homer':

all I deny is, that a poet can be said to rise and sink when all that he, as a poet, can do, is perfectly well done; when he is perfectly sound and good, that is, perfect as a poet, in the level regions of his subject as well as in its elevated regions.

(p. 186)

4

Genre theory II:
the twentieth century

Forms may be regarded as institutional imperatives which both
coerce and are in turn coerced by the writer.

(Norman Holmes Pearson,
'Literary forms and types; or, a defence of Polonius')

Strolling along a rainy Dublin street, Joyce's Stephen Dedalus is
discoursing about art:

The image, it is clear, must be set between the mind or senses of
the artist himself and the mind or senses of others. If you bear
this in memory you will see that art necessarily divides itself into
three forms progressing from one to the next. These forms are:
the lyrical form, the form wherein the artist presents his image
in immediate relation to himself; the epical form, the form
wherein he presents his image in mediate relation to himself and
to others; the dramatic form, the form wherein he presents his
image in immediate relation to others.

(*A Portrait of the Artist as a Young Man*, pp. 213–14)

But Stephen's companion is singularly unsympathetic to these and
similar meditations:

—What do you mean, Lynch asked surlily, by prating about
beauty and the imagination in this miserable God-forsaken
island?

(p. 215)

Many twentieth-century critics have explored the nature of genre
with no less intensity than that manifested by Stephen Dedalus;

and many others have rejected the relevance of genre with no less vehemence than that expressed by Lynch.

We have seen that their various attitudes to genre mirror the larger distinctions between the different currents of literary criticism that succeeded each other in previous centuries. Such attitudes also provide a touchstone to the coexisting and competing schools of our own period. The tools that modern readers adopt to study genre differ significantly from critic to critic, and differ in ways that highlight the roots of their critical assumptions: predictably enough, the structuralists borrow linguistic methods, a scholar like Rosalie Colie bases her conclusions on traditional historical scholarship, Northrop Frye's debt to Jungian psychology is evident throughout his work and so on. The issues about genre that interest the proponents of contemporary schools of criticism are also varied, and varied in ways that manifest underlying credos about the nature of literature: one can, say, play the taxonomic preoccupations of a neo-Aristotelian like Elder Olson against the philosophical concerns of an Emil Staiger or the sociological orientation of the later Lukács.

*　　*　　*

It was the Italian philosopher Benedetto Croce who most influentially expressed the reservations about genre that are echoed in the work of many subsequent critics of this century. Adopting a definition of the creative process that owes much to romantic thought, he argues in his *Estetica* that knowledge takes two forms. The intuitive, which is achieved through the imagination, consists of knowledge about individual phenomena and produces images. The logical, in contrast, is obtained through the intellect; it concentrates on universal phenomena and produces not images but concepts. The act of creating art and the act of responding to it exemplify the intuitive – or should do so.

According to Croce's system, generic categories distort the reactions of the reader who is attempting to apply them to a work of art: they lead him to move from an intuitive to a logical response to that work, and the two reactions cannot coexist. In any event, he maintains, classifying literature according to its genre is a denial of its very nature and hence does violence not only to the sensibility of the critic but also to the object he is studying. Every true work breaks generic laws, and so establishing formal classifications is not only an irrelevant response but also a dangerous one:

> The books in a library must be arranged in one way or another. This used generally to be done by a rough classification of subjects (among which the categories of miscellaneous and eccentric were not wanting); they are now generally arranged by sizes or by publishers. Who can deny the necessity and the utility of such arrangements? But what should we say if some one began seriously to seek out the literary laws of miscellanies and of eccentricities, of the Aldines or Bodonis, of shelf A or shelf B, that is to say, of those altogether arbitrary groupings whose sole object was their practical utility. Yet should any one attempt such an undertaking, he would be doing neither more nor less than those do who seek out the *aesthetic laws* which must in their belief control literary and artistic kinds.

(p. 38)

Croce's distrust of genre found many sympathizers as our century progressed. A number of subsequent critics proffered arguments quite close to his, rejecting not only genre but also any other historical approach to literature on the grounds that every work of art must be seen as unique. In addition, during the past decade certain theorists, such as Jacques Derrida, have come to emphasize the indeterminacy of the text. Even Roland Barthes, who earlier in his career pioneered structuralist literary criticism, adopts this position in his final writings, maintaining that since the reader is faced with an infinite series of conflicting signals and codes, it is almost impossible to interpret a work of literature precisely and objectively. Hence, according to readers of this persuasion, the codes that in theory might help us to read the text – including genre – are in practice virtually irrelevant. Yet other critics have argued that while genre may have been important in other periods, it plays no significant role in modern literature. 'To break the pentameter, that was the first heave', Pound announces in his *Cantos*, and many have believed that the modernists fractured generic molds no less energetically than prosodic ones.

The significance of genre has, however, been reasserted determinedly and, I would maintain, definitively, by a number of modern theorists. In fact, some of the most suggestive contemporary work on this subject takes the form of comparatively brief essays that aim to defend the concept of literary types and in the process of doing so offer thought-provoking general speculations about genre. Renato Poggioli's 'Poetics and metrics', a case in point, stresses the importance of genre in twentieth-century literature:

> even in our time every author accepts and follows a given set of presuppositions, determining and conditioning his writing at least in the realm of what is now being called 'conventional form' . . . like its ancient counterpart, modern poetics is but a system of literary *genres*.
>
> (pp. 193–4)

Poggioli goes on to argue that in our age poetic norms are transmitted through what he terms 'unwritten poetics' (that is, the assumptions about literature that have not been codified into official pronouncements). This reliance on a poetics that is unwritten but far from uninfluential is, he maintains, characteristic both of primitive eras and of those that are 'eclectic, composite, and decadent' (p. 195), while in a classical or neo-classical period the unwritten poetics will be subordinate to the official one. Even in classical ages, however, the unwritten poetics is the medium responsible for communicating the relationship between metrics and other generic norms, a relationship that he considers no less significant in our own literature than it was in Greek and Latin writing:

one of the main tasks of [the unwritten poetics] is to inter-connect a historical system of literary *genres* with a parallel system of verse forms. In brief, it is through the sanction of unwritten poetics that a given meter comes to be generally viewed as the most characteristic technical and formal instrument of a given *genre*. . . . That law can be stated by saying that the apparition of a new literary *genre* is always accompanied by the invention or the exclusive adoption by that *genre* of a definite verse form.

(p. 196)

Genre is defended on different grounds in a group of articles that appeared in the French journal *Helicon* in the late 1930s; one of the most thoughtful is Paul van Tieghem's 'La question des genres littéraires'. He writes that the notion of genres is not and cannot be dead, for it is firmly based in human psychology: 'Each emotional taste, each social or religious need is the root of a different genre which blossoms more or less happily' (p. 97). Defining literary types in terms of their relationship to the emotional needs of author and reader rather than their formal structures, he persuasively suggests that genres that seem far apart from each other in other ways should in fact be seen as allied if they 'put into play the same faculties of the authors, the same tastes of the public' (p. 99). This observation has, as we will see, the broadest of implications for studying generic evolution; in particular, it encourages us to note subterranean parallels between literary forms that may be totally different in their subject matter and their prosodic patterns.

*   *   *

Of the many theorists who accept the importance of genre, the neo-Aristotelians are perhaps the most traditional in their methods and their assumptions. So many proponents of this literary school taught at the University of Chicago that they came to be termed the Chicago School, but it is the title 'neo-Aristotelian' that neatly encapsulates their approach: they attempt to expand and refine the literary system established in the *Poetics*, often by classifying literary forms on which Aristotle himself does not offer extended commentary or by adding further distinctions to categories that he does establish. Elder Olson's 'An outline of poetic theory', for example, provides a useful summary of Aristotle's own criteria for analyzing literary forms and proceeds to extend those criteria in order to distinguish types of 'action'. He establishes four basic types: works that present a single character in a closed situation (that is, a situation in which his actions are uncomplicated by those of any other agent), such as most lyric poetry; works that show two or more characters in a closed situation; works consisting of a collection of scenes; and works consisting of a collection of episodes.

In R. S. Crane's 'The concept of plot and the plot of *Tom Jones*' we encounter a similar development of the *Poetics*. Noting that Fielding's plot has excited more admiration than analysis, he articulates a series of principles for studying narrative:

> In stating this principle for any plot, we must consider three things: (1) the general estimate we are induced to form, by signs in the work, of the moral character and deserts of the hero, as a result of which we tend, more or less ardently, to wish for him either good or bad fortune in the end; (2) the judgments we are led similarly to make about the nature of the events that actually befall the hero or seem likely to befall him, as having either painful or pleasurable consequences for him, and this in greater or less degree and permanently or temporarily; and (3) the opinions we are made to entertain concerning the degree and kind of his responsibility for what happens to him. . . . The form of a given plot is a function of the particular correlation among these three variables.
>
> (p. 632)

Behind these categories, of course, lie Aristotle's observations about the object of imitation.

★   ★   ★

The Russian formalists and the structuralists are as iconoclastic and innovative in their approach to genre – and to many other aesthetic questions as well – as the neo-Aristotelians are conservative. One reason for the self-conscious originality that characterizes both formalism and structuralism is that these two closely related schools owe much to certain developments in modern linguistics. It is far from coincidental that Roman Jakobson, a leader in these two fields of criticism was also a member of the influential Moscow Linguistic Circle.

Central in modern linguistics, and crucial in the influence of that field on formalism and structuralism, is the distinction between *langue* and *parole* formulated by Ferdinand de Saussure. The first of those terms represents the laws governing a particular language, such as the rules enumerating the prepositions determined by certain verbs; the second refers to a specific linguistic utterance, whether it be a statement in ordinary conversation or a poem. Linguistic concepts like these, as well as the underlying scientific orientation that shapes them, proved so important to the formalists and structuralists that Roman Jakobson declares, 'Poetics deals with problems of verbal structure. . . . Since linguistics is the global science of verbal structure, poetics may be regarded as an integral part of linguistics' ('Linguistics and poetics', in *Style and Language*, p. 350).

Together with the American philosopher Charles Peirce, Saussure also pioneered the field of semiotics, a subject whose insights have been adopted not only for critical analyses (including commentaries on genre), but also for everything from Marxist descriptions of fashion to psychological interpretations of human interactions. Many subsequent theorists have refined Saussure and Peirce's work, concentrating especially on providing additional or more precise terminology, but the central idea behind semiotics has remained constant. Semiotics is in its broadest sense an examination of how meaning is conveyed through signs. The sign consists of a signifier and a signified (Anglo-American critics often retain the French terms *signifiant* and *signifié*). Thus the sound of the word 'cat' is in itself merely an arbitrary noise; when, however, that signifier is applied to the animal in question (the signified), a sign is produced.

Behind the work of the Russian formalists, a school that flourished during the first three decades of this century, lie not only linguistic discoveries like those of Saussure but also a number of more local and more topical problems. The Russian formalists were reacting against what they saw as the vaguenesses and the vagaries of German idealism, as well as against the biographical critics who had enjoyed such a vogue in their own country. They also took issue with recent developments in several other disciplines; in particular, they rejected the positivist emphasis on separating the sciences from the humanities, and they sided with the futurists against the symbolists in the debate that was raging in Russian artistic circles.

This background helps to explain the formalist commitment to studying literature systematically and scientifically, as well as their contempt for evidence borrowed from other spheres, such as biography and social history. Another central principle in their essays is the tenet that literary and non-literary language differ significantly from each other; it is on the distinctly literary qualities of a work of art, which they term its 'literariness', that critical enquiry should focus.

In examining this 'literariness', they enumerate and scrutinize the units of which an artistic work is constructed, much as a modern linguist would study the grammatical units of an utterance; their earliest writings concentrated especially on sound patterns, though they subsequently also directed their attention to other elements, such as the narrative motifs catalogued in Vladimir Propp's influential study of folk tales. The formalists emphasize the need to study the functions of such literary elements rather than merely identifying them (as one writer points out, archaisms may create an elevated tone in one work but render another parodic), as well as the ways the elements interrelate within the cohesive 'system' of the work at hand.

As this summary of their methodology may suggest, there are many aspects of genre that interested the formalists, and interested them enough to generate some of the most illuminating essays on literary types written in this century. They devote considerable attention to the underlying characteristics that, as it were, inform literary forms, notably those sound patterns and arrangements of narrative units. In examining such characteristics, they adduce the concept of 'the dominant', which is the particular element of a literary type, such as its prosody, that characterizes the form and determines the other elements within it. Their studies of such issues encompass not only the genres that previous critics had concentrated on, but also many 'low' forms, like the fairy-tale; they maintain that these 'low' forms illuminate the structural patterns that they share with more serious types of literature and that, in addition, they should interest us in their own right.

Among the most stimulating writings of the formalists are their essays on generic and other literary changes, notably Jurii Tynyanov's work on the subject. It is no accident that writers who had lived through a turbulent political revolution should prove to be interested in generic revolutions and evolutions and prone to describe such changes in terms that could also be applied to political upheavals. They maintain that genres often change through what they term the 'law of contrasts'; that is, rather than enjoying a smooth and gradual evolution, a type may move abruptly from, say, the high style of sentimental literature to the reversal of that style in parody. As Tynyanov puts it, 'Any literary succession is first of all a struggle, a destruction of old values and a reconstruction of old elements' (quoted in Boris Eichenbaum, 'The theory of the formal method', in *Russian Formalist Criticism*, p. 134). Tynyanov posits another explanation for generic development in 'Rhythm as the constructive factor of verse': the conjunction or combination of one order with another may generate changes. He cites the way romantic poets adopted trimeter, previously used in comic verse, for serious poetry. Roman Jakobson is making a similar point when he observes, 'The hierarchy of artistic devices changes within the framework of a given poetic genre; the change, moreover, affects the hierarchy of poetic genres, and, simultaneously, the distribution of artistic devices among the individual genres' ('The dominant', in *Readings in Russian Poetics*, p. 85). Or, the formalists suggest, a previously unrespectable form may be canonized, a process that may lead to the increased prominence of what had been a cadet branch of the family. The changing attitudes to science fiction offer a case in point from contemporary American literature.

The Russian formalists were suppressed for political reasons in the 1930s; but many of their principles re-emerged in the work of the structuralists. For in certain regards the two schools are separated only by chronology. Both structuralist and formalist literary critics tend to ignore the issues of what has been termed 'extrinsic criticism', such as the biography of the author or the social history of his age; both concern themselves instead with analyzing elements like sound patterns and plot structures and with locating them within the system of the work as a whole. In other ways, though, structuralism is very different from the school that preceded it. In particular, where formalism so rigorously concentrates on poetic language, structuralism is an interdisciplinary movement, applying its principles in arenas that range from anthropological rites to literary texts to home furnishings. One of the chief proponents of structuralism, in fact, is the anthropologist Claude Lévi-Strauss.

Whatever their principal field of enquiry, structuralists study the underlying patterns or structures that inform the phenomenon they are examining. What interests them primarily is not overt structures like themes but rather the subterranean ones sometimes termed 'deep' structures, such as, say, a conflict between the civilized and the natural (Lévi-Strauss's famous opposition, examined in his book *Le cru et le cuit*). They repeatedly draw our attention to the similarities between patterns like these and linguistic ones.

Emphasizing 'system' even more than the Russian formalists, structuralists characteristically focus on the interrelationships between the elements in whatever activity they are analyzing. The relationship that they consider most significant and most recurrent is the binary one – in anthropological data this may be the conflict between static and dynamic forces, in literary the opposition between types of concord and discord and so on.

Theories like these breed a radically different approach to genre than that of, say, the neo-Aristotelians. Rather than classifying literary forms according to overt and semantic characteristics like the nature of their heroes, structuralists are prone to define a literary type by its underlying pattern – the rhetorical figure or the linguistic usage or even the type of discourse in ordinary life that it most resembles. Adapting the formalist emphasis on what Claudio Guillén terms 'literature as system', structuralists tend to study the interrelationship between different elements in a genre (say, how the repetitions in its plot mirror a recurrent figure of speech that is also based on repetition) and between one genre and other elements in the same literary system.

Many of these concerns are manifest in the work of the Czech structuralist Jan Mukarovský. Several of the essays in his seminal *The Word and Verbal Art* explore an issue that had intrigued the formalists as well: the distinction between the monologic and the dialogic. In 'On poetic language', for instance, he argues for expanding our definition of the dialogic to encompass works that, while lacking the presence of two distinct speakers, manifest certain characteristics that he considers closely related to that one; those characteristics, analyzed at length in 'Two studies of dialogue', include concessive relations ('despite', 'none the less' and so on) and evaluative oppositions ('good-bad'). The distinction between monologue and dialogue that he shapes has many literary implications – indeed, he goes so far as to assert that it is a basic polarity of all literary activity – but what is especially important to our purposes is the relevance of his distinction to genre. Predictably, he suggests that lyric and narrative are primarily monologic and drama primarily dialogic, but he proceeds to qualify that classification with a number of provisos and refinements, stressing throughout that in many works the two modes interpenetrate and interact.

Jan Mukarovský is also very concerned with literary evolution. One of its sources, he suggests, is the process in which an author turns to a genre other than the one in which he normally writes and reshapes it by introducing into it some of the patterns associated with the literary form to which he is more accustomed. (Shakespeare's reinterpretation of romance is a case in point from our own literary tradition.) Many of his general observations about literary models and literary influence, such as his reminder that younger poets can influence older ones as well as vice versa, have important ramifications for the study of genre.

Another structuralist critic, the contemporary theorist Tzvetan Todorov, also demonstrates the close link between the structuralists and the Russian formalists who preceded them. For in more senses than one he is responsible for making the work of Tynyanov accessible to us: his anthology, *Théorie de la littérature*, includes two of his predecessor's most important essays, while many of his own observations on generic evolution develop those of Tynyanov. Asserting the continuing relevance of genre, Todorov refutes both the claim that it is in general a misleading concept and the assumption that it no longer figures significantly in modern literature. Genre remains important, he declares, even in the case of works that transgress generic norms:

> For there to be a transgression, the norm must be apparent. Moreover, it is doubtful that contemporary literature is entirely exempt from generic distinctions; it is only that these distinctions no longer correspond to the notions bequeathed by the literary theories of the past . . . failing to recognize the existence of genres is equivalent to claiming that a literary work does not bear any relationship to already existing works. Genres are precisely those relay-points by which the work assumes a relation with the universe of literature.
>
> (*The Fantastic*, p. 8)

More tendentiously, he argues for a radical expansion of the definition of genre: the intrinsic abstractness of language, he maintains, makes every statement about an individual work in some sense a statement about genre.

The subtitle of Tzvetan Todorov's *The Fantastic* is in fact *A Structural Approach to a Literary Genre*, and both there and elsewhere he enumerates the principles on which he believes genre should be studied. Northrop Frye, he suggests, makes the mistake of schematizing literary forms on the basis of non-literary qualities like the moral worth of the hero or the nature of his environment. The assertion that such qualities are not literary, of course, clarifies Tzvetan Todorov's poetics as much or more than Frye's, highlighting as it does the structuralist presupposition that underlying structural patterns are of more significance than traditional concerns like theme and character. Rather than focusing on the literary elements that interest Frye, he suggests we should interpret all observable aspects of the work as the manifestation of 'an abstract construct which is a mental construction and which sets in opposition, let us say, the static and dynamic' (p. 17).

Like so many other modern theorists, he stresses the element of conflict in generic change, the way each serious work (as opposed to a merely popular one) is in some sense in rebellion against previously established generic norms. He is also concerned with broader historical patterns of generic evolution. At several points he emphasizes the danger of oversimplifying our study of generic characteristics and changes; he reminds us, for example, that each new literary form, unlike each new biological one, modifies its species. Another danger in studying genre, this critic suggests, is assuming that one form evolves from another in a neat and orderly pattern, consisting of a mere rearrangement of the same elements:

> Unfortunately for logic, genres are not constituted in conformity with structural descriptions; a new genre is created around an element which was not obligatory in the old one: the two encode different elements. For this reason the poetics of

classicism was wasting its time seeking a logical classification of genres.

(The Poetics of Prose, pp. 47–8)

Jonathan Culler's *Structuralist Poetics* addresses the dual problem of summarizing and evaluating central issues in pre-existing structuralist criticism, notably the question of its relationship to linguistics, while also formulating the principles on which a structuralist poetics should be based. His commitment to the significance of genre is reflected in the prominent place he assigns the subject in his study: he devotes one long section to arguing for the validity of generic classifications and also discusses literary types from a number of other angles throughout the book. The central principles informing the volume help to explain this emphasis on genre: while acknowledging the importance of linguistics, he repeatedly asserts that we cannot grasp all the meaning of a text by studying its linguistic patterns, as certain structuralists had claimed. We must instead recognize that several external codes and systems, including the generic, influence both author and reader:

> To write a poem or a novel is immediately to engage with a literary tradition or at the very least with a certain idea of the poem or the novel. The activity is made possible by the existence of the genre, which the author can write against, certainly, whose conventions he may attempt to subvert, but which is none the less the context within which his activity takes place, as surely as the failure to keep a promise is made possible by the institution of promising.
>
> (p. 116)

In other words, all works must be read in relation to the literary system in which they occur, just as all linguistic utterances must be interpreted according to the rules of their *langue*.

Jonathan Culler proceeds to discuss some of the functions of genre and in so doing demonstrates the role he believes genre systems should assume in a poetics based on structuralist principles. He stresses that our approach to genre should not be merely taxonomic; developing the formalist concern for function in terms of the preoccupation with the reader that characterizes so much contemporary criticism, Culler argues that what we should study about genre is not its form as such but rather how elements of that form govern the reading of the work. One such function genre can assume, he suggests, is to establish the *vraisemblable* (that concept has many meanings in structuralist criticism, but the one most relevant here is what is permitted to happen in a work of art). Thus, to choose a very simple example, dragons are alive and well in the world of romance but hardly conceivable in a no less stylized form like the spy novel; or, as we saw earlier, the murderer in my hypothetical detective novel could not be a ghost.

Structuralist Poetics also includes analyses of two particular genres, the novel and the lyric, and here the author questions certain common clichés about those two forms, arguing, for example, that the lyric is marked not by the sense of the immediate and the personal that many critics have attributed to it but rather by distance and impersonality. He attempts to substantiate this point by describing linguistic patterns in lyric, such as the use of deictics (markers like 'this' and 'here').

The term 'formalism' describes a rather different critical approach when applied to Anglo-American critics instead of their Russian predecessors. By and large Anglo-American formalists are far less concerned with literary theory in general and linguistics in particular; by and large, they have devoted far less attention to the evolution of literary systems. New Criticism, with its advocacy of an intense examination of the individual text, is the extreme instance of these tendencies. Hence while writers who would be styled formalists in England and America do not ignore genre, neither do they study it as frequently and as intensely as their namesakes in Russia.

One notable exception is Rosalie Colie, much of whose literary criticism emphasizes literary forms, especially genres. In *The Resources of Kind*, a brief but very illuminating book based on lectures she delivered shortly before her death, she focuses on the historical background of genre theory in the English Renaissance. *Shakespeare's Living Art* opens with an emphatic reminder that literary forms exercised a shaping influence on the works of writers, especially Shakespeare himself, and should therefore enjoy a similar influence on the thought of his critics:

> Forms are those *schemata* which by their cultural accessibility ready us to take in whatever we do take in of an environment, our own lived environment, the environment of another place and time, the environment of a given work of art.
>
> Obviously, then, forms are crucial in the translation of ideas, including aesthetic ideas, from mind to mind.... An unmediated vision cannot be communicated. ... Since Shakespeare's work is preeminently mediated and mediating, speaking as it has to so many kinds of men, I need not argue for the presence and importance of forms in his work; we all know they are there. What I must argue for, with some determination, is the presence of 'norms' in that work, since he of all authors seems freest in breaking patterns.
>
> (pp. 10–11)

Shakespeare's Living Art proceeds to examine the norms and the forms that play so crucial a role in that author's achievement. Thus, for example, Rosalie Colie traces the ways Shakespeare's sonnets highlight the 'real' implications behind the conventions of their genre, and she demonstrates how and why the playwright dismantles in *Troilus and Cressida* literary norms very like those he elsewhere emulates. Her suggestive points about the connections between the sonnet and the epigram, also adumbrated in *The Resources of Kind*, parallel Claudio Guillén's statements about the interrelationships between genres, notably the complex dialogue between what he terms 'genre and counter-genre'. In one of the most illuminating sections of the book, the author analyzes the 'forms' in *Love's Labour's Lost*, encompassing in these observations patterns ranging from *commedia dell'arte* character types to rhetorical figures, and examining how such forms function as 'pointers to personality' (p. 44). As her analysis of this and several other plays demonstrates, one reason the volume is so thought provoking is that it repeatedly places Shakespeare's experiments with genre in the context of his work on and with other conventions, including such seemingly diverse ones as topoi, epigrammatic observations and traditional intellectual debates.

*   *   *

While it is quite possible to classify many of the critics whom we have encountered so far in terms of their predominant intellectual orientation, such an attempt breaks down when we turn to Northrop Frye. His alliance with Aristotle is so close that he too might almost be called a neo-Aristotelian, were he not related to so many other schools as well: much of his work on generic evolution develops the ideas of the Russian formalists, his concern for interrelating and interpenetrating patterns recalls the structuralists, and his debt to Jung is so profound that he and his followers are sometimes termed archetypal critics. What this amalgam of influences produces is one of the most original and sweeping – and, as those adjectives might lead us to predict, one of the most controversial – theories of genre developed this century.

Underlying much of Frye's writing is the conviction that the central work of the literary critic is to classify the opus of literature. Criticism is to literature, he suggests in *Anatomy of Criticism*, as history is to action or philosophy is to wisdom. This conception of criticism helps to explain why he, like the formalists and structuralists, challenges the positivist division of the sciences and humanities, stressing instead their underlying methodological affinity:

If criticism exists, it must be an examination of literature in terms of a conceptual framework derivable from an inductive survey of the literary field. The word 'inductive' suggests some sort of scientific procedure. What if criticism is a science as well as an art? . . . The presence of science in any subject changes its character from the casual to the causal, from the random and intuitive to the systematic.

(*Anatomy of Criticism*, p. 7)

Such a concept of literary studies carries with it many assumptions about both the work of art and the critic who analyzes it. Literature will be expected to form as clear and as consistent a pattern as, say, the feline family; Frye writes of the 'assumption of total coherence' (p. 16) that lies behind his theories. The role of the critic is to explore and to explicate the pattern, the system of literature, but never to pass value judgments on it, a point on which Frye continues to insist in his other writings as well. In effect he is seconding Roman Jakobson's assertion that to term someone a literary critic is as nonsensical as calling someone a grammatical critic would be.

Since literature is a system that lends itself to scientific analysis, literary forms are evidently of prime importance to the critic. Such forms are, of course, of no less significance to the writer; it is in fact the prescriptions of those types, not the predilections of his own character, that shape the work of art. As Frye puts it in *A Natural Perspective*, his study of Shakespeare's comedies and romances, there is 'no passage in Shakespeare's plays . . . which cannot be explained entirely in terms of its dramatic function and context . . . nothing which owes its existence to Shakespeare's desire to "say" something' (p. 36).

Anatomy of Criticism offers several interlocking categorizations of literature; these various systems are in turn shaped by and reflected in the patterns of archetypal imagery that concern Frye so much. One system is that which Frye calls modes, a classification that develops Aristotle's concept of the object of imitation. The hero's 'power of action', he argues, may be classified in one of five ways: (i) If he is superior in kind to other men and the environment, the story will be a myth; (ii) If he is superior in degree to other men and to the environment, the mode is romance; (iii) If he is superior in degree to other men but not to his environment, the work is high mimetic, the mode of most tragic drama and epic poetry; (iv) If he is superior neither to other men nor to his environment, the mode is low mimetic, that of most comedy and of realist fiction; (v) If he is inferior to us, the mode is ironic.

Another category established by Frye is the 'mythos', an archetypal plot whose name is borrowed from the Greek word Aristotle uses for plot. These mythoi are broader than, or prior to, the usual literary forms. Frye distinguishes four of them, each corresponding to a season: the comic (spring), the romantic (summer), the tragic (autumn) and the satiric (winter). The link between the mythoi and the seasons exemplifies the way Frye reinterprets the Aristotelian concept of mimesis throughout his study: rather than examining how an artistic work may mirror actual events, he uncovers broad patterns in the world of art, such as narrative structures, that correspond to equally broad patterns in the world of nature and to myths in the customary sense of the term.

Aristotle's 'manner of imitation' is redefined by Frye and emerges as another general category: this he labels 'genre', though he anticipates some of his critics by freely admitting that he uses this and a few other terms in several different ways in *Anatomy of Criticism*. He stresses that genres in this sense of the term are intrinsic and basic to the works in question; even if drama is printed rather than acted, for example, it still adheres to the same genre. Applying his concept of genres to the triad, he distinguishes types of narrative, arguing that 'epos' preserves the convention of recitation even if it is not recited, while 'fiction', in contrast, is the genre of the printed page.

Though these are the systems of classification in *Anatomy of Criticism* most directly relevant to genre, Frye's taxonomy does not, of course, stop here. He is especially interested in three central patterns of symbolism and imagery: the apocalyptic, the demonic and the analogical. He also traces a number of subdivisions within his categories of literary forms. One such pattern involves a radical redefinition of the customary division between literary and sub-literary or non-literary forms: he distinguishes two broad types of writing, the fictional (which includes everything that tells a story and has internal characters) and the thematic (in which the author and the reader are the only characters), though he notes that many works of art in fact include both types. The thematic, Frye asserts, numbers among its strange bedfellows lyrics, essays, didactic poetry and oratory.

Like many of the critics who preceded him, Frye sees genres as describing a cycle of ascendancy and decline. Literature as a whole, he suggests, passes through the five modes, with the cycle reverting to the mythic at the end; it is currently at the ironic phase, with some signs of the impending return to the mythic. This circular pattern does not, however, represent a system of decline and improvement. The genres, too, go through periods of ascendancy. Nor do individual literary types adhere to fixed places in the system; Frye is especially interested in the ways certain types or certain works within a type may move between different points on his spectrum.

Throughout *Anatomy of Criticism* Frye is concerned to trace the different functions that the same literary element may assume or the different guises it may wear in each of the several phases of his system. Thus, for example, in high mimetic tragedy the elements of pity and fear operate as moral judgments; in low mimetic tragedy, their main function is to produce sensation, especially pathos. The benevolent withdrawing and returning figure in comedy is transformed into the character whose decree produces the tragic action in tragedy – God the Father in *Paradise Lost* or the ghost in *Hamlet*. In romance, the comparable figure is the Jungian 'old wise man'; after citing Prospero and Merlin as typical incarnations, Frye offers the suggestive observation that Arthur, although not old, assumes this role in *The Faerie Queene*. Similarly, the tragic parallel to such comedic characters as Malvolio is a type of plaindealer like Kent or Horatio, a character who resists the tragic conclusion in much the same way his comedic counterpart resists the denouement in his own genre.

Frye also examines the ways his mythoi change. Comedy, he argues, goes through several phases:

> These five phases of comedy may be seen as a sequence of stages in the life of a redeemed society. Purely ironic comedy exhibits this society in its infancy. . . . Quixotic comedy exhibits it in adolescence, still too ignorant of the ways of the world to impose itself. In the third phase it comes to maturity and triumphs; in the fourth it is already mature and established. In the fifth it is part of a settled order which has been there from the beginning, an order which takes on an increasingly religious cast and seems to be drawing away from human experience altogether. . . . At this point we realize that the crudest of Plautine comedy-formulas has much the same *structure* as the central Christian myth itself, with its divine son appeasing the wrath of a father and redeeming what is at once a society and a bride.
>
>   At this point too comedy proper enters its final or sixth phase, the phase of the collapse and disintegration of the comic society. . . . Secret and sheltered places, forests in moonlight, secluded valleys, and happy islands become more prominent, as does the *penseroso* mood of romance.

(p. 185)

One sign of Frye's significance in modern criticism is the number of addenda or corrigenda *Anatomy of Criticism* has inspired ever since its publication in 1957. In *The Nature of Narrative*, for instance, Robert Scholes and Robert Kellogg borrow Frye's methods and expand or refine many of his classifications. Thus they posit and develop a distinction between empirical and fictional writing, a distinction that corresponds to two branches of epic. The empirical category is in turn divided into two branches, historical (for example history writing and biography) and mimetic (for example autobiography). Similarly, the fictional is subdivided into the romantic, or works shaped by an aesthetic impulse, and the didactic, or works shaped by an intellectual or moral impulse. In the novel, they maintain, empirical and fictional writing are being reunited, just as they were once synthesized in the epic. Other scholars, too, have refined Frye's work, often by proffering new terms for the ones he uses or by augmenting the classifications he establishes.

*   *   *

Contemporary German critics have developed several significant theories of genre, a number of which represent an application of modern linguistics to the problems about the triad that had intrigued so many of their countrymen during the nineteenth century. In her important study *Die Logik der Dichtung*, Käte Hamburger posits a fundamental distinction between epic and dramatic on the one hand and lyric on the other: the former modes convey a sense of unreality and the latter a sense of reality. To support this dichotomy, she isolates several qualities in narrative that, she maintains, create the impression of fictionality. First, the past tense in fiction does not suggest the past as we know it but rather a situation in the present; when we read, 'John walked into the room', we do not assume, as we would if we encountered the same preterite in another type of writing, that the action being described occurred prior to one in our own world. Fictionality is also established, she suggests, by allusions to fictional space. Thus 'John walked over there' refers to a spatial construct within the novel itself.

Reinterpreting the concern with *Erlebnis*, or subjective experience, that had preoccupied German romantic critics, Käte Hamburger argues that we read a lyric (or a novel narrated in the first person, which she classifies with lyric) as 'real utterance' (*Wirklichkeitssaussage*). Such works offer no internal evidence that allows us to judge whether or not they are literally true, she maintains, and in support of that contention cites a poem by Novalis that would be read as a lyric if we encountered it in a collection of lyrics, but would instead be interpreted as a hymn, with the 'I' referring to the congregation collectively, if it were encountered in a religious service.

Another German critic, Emil Staiger, also reinterprets the triad, though his perspective on it is very different from that of Käte Hamburger. Like many other modern critics, he is concerned to distinguish particular works from a more abstract notion of modal attitudes; a lyric poem may be lyrical, he emphasizes, but it is not necessarily so. Indeed, he goes so far as to suggest that our concept of the modes may not be based on literary works at all: it is possible that the experience of looking at a landscape, say, lies behind the lyrical. He stresses, too, that most literary works contain components of all three modes, though they may well be colored by a predominance of one.

He proceeds to effect a number of parallels that illuminate the three modes, variously drawing his comparisons from linguistics and philosophy. Applying the theories of the philosopher Ernst Cassirer, he asserts that the lyrical, epical and dramatic correspond to the syllable, the word and the sentence. Like a syllable, the lyrical is an expressive form that carries no meaning and fulfills no purpose; like a word, the epical defines an object; like a sentence, the dramatic is concerned with the relationship between subject and verb, or actor and action. These comparisons demonstrate a point that concerns Emil Staiger particularly both in *Grundbegriffe der Poetik* and some of his other work as well, the interrelationship of all three modes. He goes on to argue that the triad embodies the three stages of man's life. The lyrical, which is associated with the sensual, is the form of childhood; the epic, associated with the representative, corresponds to youth; and the dramatic, associated with the conceptual, is the mode of maturity. The three modes differ, too, in their relationship to time; here Staiger adduces Heidegger's theories of time to rebut the conventional clichés about the immediacy of the lyrical. Instead, he asserts, it is related to past events, while the epic is more closely linked to the present.

5
Conclusion

> An inquiry into the nature of the *genres* . . . ramifies out in every
> direction, and involves one's attitude not merely towards literature
> but also towards life.
>
> (Irving Babbitt, *The New Laokoon*)

The author of a book on genre who emphasizes the importance of
that subject and stresses the need for further work in it courts the
same accusations that might be leveled at a military officer calling
for a larger defense budget. Even the most unprejudiced of
observers, however, might well urge that readers and critics of
many persuasions take a greater interest in genre. The increasing
availability of the seminal essays by the Russian formalists should
alone provide an impetus for more work in the field.

As we have seen, the important theoretical writings of the past
few decades adumbrate some directions that future research might
fruitfully take; but they also exemplify some pitfalls that future
research should avoid. Both their respect for scientific methods
and their adoption of linguistic models have encouraged certain
readers to view generic codes far too deterministically, to assume
that generic norms not only affect but also effect the decisions of
the writer and the responses of the reader. In his stimulating but
controversial *Validity in Interpretation*, for example, E. D. Hirsch
argues that the meaning of the text is essentially the one intended
by its author and cites genre as one way that meaning is conveyed.
Critical studies of literary types as well as those types themselves
may describe cyclical patterns, and it is apparent that we are now
faced with problems analogous to those occasioned by the use of
evolutionary terminology a few generations ago: once again we are
prone to believe that generic patterns may be predicted with

certainty once we have classified the forms and codified their norms. To be sure, several voices have been raised against this assumption – one thinks especially of Tzvetan Todorov's salutary emphasis on the complexity of generic development – but it remains a common tendency.

Genres are frequently compared to elements of *langue*, such as grammatical rules, or to a *parole* that can become *langue* when it is further established. Such analogies are often apt, but we will substitute for that misleadingly deterministic interpretation of genre a sanative respect for its variety and flexibility if, returning from a different angle to a parallel we explored previously, we adduce as yet another analogue, the idiolect. Slang or a local patois exemplify idiolects in the relevant sense of the term – that is the speech of a sub-group or subculture, the expanded definition advocated by such theorists as Barthes. The rules of slang, like those of genres, can be modified rapidly without threatening the whole system or confusing its adherents. A speaker may abandon certain usages of his local dialect, just as he may ignore or modify generic norms, without delivering a statement that is, as it were, ungrammatical.

Viewing genre and genres too deterministically has also led to oversimplifying readers' responses to them. We need to remember that, as several critics have observed, generic codes frequently function like a tone of voice rather than a more clearcut signal: they provide one interpretation of the meaning of the text, they direct our attention to the parts of it that are especially significant, but they do not and they cannot offer an infallible key to its meaning. One may make a serious statement in a light tone, just as one may invoke generic conventions ironically; one may express nuances of feeling – or deliberately confuse one's listeners about one's feelings – by moving rapidly from tone to tone, just as one may include elements of the pastoral in the heroic. We should remind ourselves, too, that the reader's reactions to genre do not necessarily follow a pattern that might be codified as 'If / Then', as many critics have assumed ('If it is a *Bildungsroman*, then x, y and z will be present'). Often that pattern might more accurately be formulated as 'What if / Then probably' ('What if the genre of this work is the *Bildungsroman*? Then probably the hero will test out a series of alternative father figures, though of course this may just be one of the few *Bildungsromane* where that pattern does not operate').

'Reader response criticism', that study of the audience's reactions that is currently much in vogue, might profitably investigate two aspects of reading that render our interpretations of generic signals far more ambivalent and far more ambiguous than we are prone to admit. The first is that the process of reading is often in fact a process of re-reading. For we seldom simply peruse an important work once through; instead, we may re-read the same poem or story several times at the same sitting, we may turn back to a previous passage in a novel when it is echoed by the passage with which we are currently engaged and so on. And, of course, we often return at a later date to a text we have previously encountered. Hence our initial experience with a particular passage should not be emphasized at the expense of subsequent experiences, as it often is in reader response criticism: that preliminary reading is no more significant in our interpretation of a work than the thousand visions and revisions that succeed it.

What this means is that the process of reacting to generic signals is seldom a simple and linear one. Admittedly, sometimes we merely start out with no idea about the work's genre, arrive at a satisfactory decision about it, and respond to the rest of the work accordingly. Often, however, even on our first reading we will reach a preliminary hypothesis about genre, bear it in mind as we glance back over earlier passages, and re-read the whole work in the light of our assumptions about its literary form. In doing so we will typically note both further evidence of the work's relationship to that type and previously unobserved deviations from the model. When we return to a text at a later date, in some instances our impressions about its genre will still be tentative hypotheses. Or, alternatively, we may re-read it with a firm assessment of its genre in mind. If, so as often happens, we then encounter ways in which it violates the norms of that genre, or contains significant motifs from other genres as well, these discoveries will be all the more startling because they conflict with our comfortable presuppositions. In other words, that initial 'What if / Then probably' pattern is sometimes repeated as we read and re-read, sometimes succeeded by a series of further qualifications and amplifications. To borrow the expression that Stephen Pepper applies to the visual arts in his study *The Basis of Criticism in the Arts*, our subsequent experiences of the work are 'funded' by previous ones.

But it is on the issue of generic expectations that a more subtle analysis of the reader's responses could help us most. One reason we need to examine this question further is that we are still prone to consider such expectations in an absolute and an ahistorical way: the epic engenders this set of expectations, drawing-room comedy that set and so on. Instead, we should acknowledge and scrutinize the ways generic expectations may intersect with other expectations and hence be intensified or undercut – or even both at once – by a whole series of signals that have nothing to do with genre directly. The most obvious but hardly the least important signal is our knowledge of the age: recognizing that the work at hand is the product of a period keenly conscious of decorum will surely intensify our generic expectations. The work itself may either reinforce or weaken those expectations by its implicit attitudes to other conventions; the fact that *Troilus and Cressida* mocks the Trojan myth makes us less surprised when generic norms are inverted. The most intriguing influence on generic expectations (and, indeed, on some other aspects of literary interpretation) is, however, what we might term authorial expectations: what we know of the writer's previous work in that genre and of his general attitudes to tradition will shape the presuppositions with which we approach his work. Thus our authorial expectations will further complicate our generic ones in the case of the passages from *The Jew of Malta* analyzed in Chapter 2: while Marlowe's generic signals prepare us to encounter the conventions of a given form, our knowledge of his characteristic iconoclasm – rhetorical, intellectual and personal – simultaneously puts us on edge and hence prepares us to notice his deviations from the very expectations he has so carefully established.

An overly deterministic interpretation of genre is one of several causes for another problem in contemporary theoretical work on the subject: critics of many orientations, divided on other issues, have conspired in the assassination of the writer himself. They suggest, for example, that the author's meaning is essentially determined by the code he invokes, or they emphasize the reader's reactions to the text to the exclusion of the writer who created it. Some of the theorists who underestimate the author's role are doing so because they also underestimate the extent to which a writer can reshape all the codes, generic and otherwise, that he has inherited. Even more fundamental an objection to discounting the author is the obvious but too often neglected fact that the writer must decide which literary form to adopt from among the many available to him. Without reverting to the simplistic criticism that alleges that a playwright composes tragedies when 'in the depths' and so on, we may fairly note that there are patterns and predilections in his sensibility that lead him to select one literary form over another and that, *pace* Frye, he may be using that very choice to 'say' something. When, for instance, Arthur Miller evokes tragic patterns in *Death of a Salesman*, he is inviting us to note both differences and similarities between classical and modern tragedy. Spenser's adoption of one key characteristic that distinguishes romance from epic, the interweaving of multiple plots and hence multiple heroes, reflects his assumption that, as Donne puts it, to reach truth we 'about must, and about must go': no single hero, or at least no human one, is capable of solving all problems single-handedly or singlemindedly. At times, too, it is not the content or tone of a genre that determines the author's decision to write within it but rather a subtle factor like his admiration for the other poets who have worked with it – but even, or especially, in these instances the choice can be revealing.

Structuralism has exacerbated a longstanding and very prevalent tendency in literary studies: critics expect to encounter consistent patterns in what they are studying, whether it be an individual work or a total literary culture, and train their students in this expectation. But in studying genre, like many other literary issues, we should also anticipate a significant degree of inconsistency: a particular element of a literary system may fill a function that could instead have been filled by another element and in so doing free that second element to operate in a very different way. Pound's decision to cast the *Cantos* in the form of an epic and hence to associate his poem with the sense of scope and the respect for tradition normally ascribed to epic may well have encouraged him to experiment with prosody and grammar. Certain functions those systems might have served, such as establishing the author's debt to tradition and building a sense of order, were already being met. The fact that Renaissance poets like Sidney were so sedulously following classical rules and norms when they employed quantitative meter and rhetorical figures may well have made them more willing to ignore those rules when approaching certain untraditional genres.

The main effect of both formalism and structuralism on our study of genre can and should be positive. Anglo-American criticism has, as yet, been influenced comparatively little by the ideas about genre proposed by these two schools. This may be attributed in part to the relative inaccessibility of some of the texts, in part to the longstanding and legendary pragmatism that shapes English criticism and at least influences its American counterpart, and in part to the support that pragmatic distrust of critical theory has received from what has been viewed as the obscurantism of structuralism. A *détente* and even a *rapprochement* are called for. The mainstream of Anglo-American criticism has much to learn from – and much to offer to – theories like those articulated by the Russian formalists. Theoretical work on genre needs to be informed, in both senses of that term, by more attention to particular works, and vice versa.

One of the central tasks Anglo-American critics have set

themselves, the description and evaluation of specific works and authors, would benefit from an increased attention to genre and genre theory. Modern literature offers a number of instances of this truth (and in so doing reminds us yet again of the continuing importance of genre even to contemporary writers). Robert Lowell's death is, of course, prompting retrospective studies of his *œuvre*, and some of the questions we might pose about the writer who will indubitably prove to be one of the greatest poets of our century are in fact generic. In what ways and for what reasons does he experiment with the sonnet? Why does he in a sense reverse the pattern described in the pseudo-Virgilian introduction to the *Aeneid*, abandoning or at the very least modifying the epic strains of his earliest poetry in favor of a verse that is both in a lower key and in what have historically been considered lower genres? What links, if any, can we find between his religious conversions and de-conversions and the genres he uses? In addition to examining how our insights into genre illuminate his *œuvre*, we might in turn ask what broad generalizations his work prompts about the genres themselves.

Several modern novelists invite similar questions. It is useful to study the seemingly radical changes in Doris Lessing's canon in terms of the cyclical shifts between ironic and mythic charted by Northrop Frye. And a recent and very promising first novel, Mary Gordon's *Final Payments*, is illuminated when we read it in relation to the *Bildungsroman*. Having nursed her invalid father for eleven years, the heroine, Isabel, faces after his death many of the situations that the protagonist in a *Bildungsroman* experiences. She leaves her father's house and its constrained world; she redefines her relationship to a whole series of father figures and one very influential surrogate mother; she takes a job and encounters corruption in this and many other arenas; and she con-fronts her long dormant sexuality. The implicit but evident com-parisons with the *Bildungsroman* hero, who typically undergoes such developments at a much earlier age and a much slower pace, highlight the oddity of her decision to devote eleven years to her parent and hence encourage us to think further about the subtly connected network of factors that led her to do so. In many other regards, too, observing the parallels with the *Bildungsroman* crystallizes implications behind this novel; the *Bildungsroman* hero, for example, typically leaves a provincial town or the countryside for the city, whereas in Isabel's case her father's home, though in a borough of New York City, acquires a suggestively comparable provinciality from the religious and ethnic narrowness that he cultivates.

What has been termed extrinsic criticism (the study of literary works in relation to non-literary factors like social and political movements) would also benefit from more attention to genre. Despite the assertions of the Russian formalists, not only literary but also extra-literary systems – political, social, religious and so on – contribute significantly to the shaping of literary forms. We all recognize, for instance, that Queen Elizabeth I's self-conscious imitation of a Petrarchan mistress enhanced the popularity of the sonnet. Perhaps the evident aging of that queen, the most prominent and most public of all Petrarchan mistresses, as well as the dynastic problems generated by her suitably Petrarchan chastity, are in turn among the causes of the decline of the love sonnet.

When we extend our concepts of genre to include non-literary parallels and even redactions in popular culture – yet another task that demands to be done, though with great caution – we may discover further illuminating interrelationships between generic and social patterns. In the Western, for example, we sometimes encounter what might loosely but profitably be considered epic elements (such as the hero who is founding a society and the conflict between the temptations of love and the demands of war); but the distrust of the sheriff in particular and the established forces of law in general leads us to speculate about the ways political credos may be influencing and even subverting epic motifs. Similarly, in not only their literary but also their cinematic incarnations the Superman and James Bond stories include many romance motifs. Both feature a vigorous hero who undertakes a quest armed with a magical weapon, as well as a villain or villains associated with darkness from whom the society must be rescued; and both exemplify Frye's observation that romance is the literary form closest to the wish-fulfillment dream.

Equally suggestive are links between genres and what we might term social motifs or, alternatively, myths in the broad sense of that word (that is, not necessarily stories about gods and heroes but rather the ideas, shared by many members of a culture, that express the society's underlying values). These motifs or myths frequently participate in or even assume the functions of genres. Thus we know that medieval references both to Eden and to the heavenly paradise, which the earthly garden was seen to prefigure, often draw on literary and pictorial pastoral traditions. But it is likely that the connection between the myth of paradise and pastoral goes even deeper than that in medieval culture: the very concept of the earthly and heavenly paradises probably filled some functions of the pastoral genre during that period, providing, for example, a world elsewhere that could be contrasted with the corruptions of everyday society. Two myths common in Tudor England, the idea of Trojan descent and what is generally termed the Tudor myth, not only are epic in the loose, popular sense but also fill psychological functions reminiscent of those of epic literature: they invite the society to celebrate its own achievements, and they suggest an order and purposefulness in history, even while fully acknowledging its countervailing propensity for chaos.

It is above all in the traditional field of literary history that genre and genre theory can and should play an increased role. Literary historians too often merely repeat the conventional wisdom about genre – that the early seventeenth century abandoned the long poem, that the Augustan period was the age *par excellence* for satire and so on – rather than look more closely at these and other generic patterns. One of the most fruitful ways to examine the nature of particular periods and the changes from one era to another is to study why certain literary forms, such as epic and romance, flourish during some ages and not others and how a particular genre interacts with the other literary forms and aesthetic attitudes of its day. Claudio Guillén's important work on such issues is mainly confined to continental literature; but in his practice of exploring these broad questions, and exploring them by focusing on the nuances of particular texts, we find a model that Anglo-American critics might well emulate.

Because of both its longevity and its variety, pastoral provides one of the best examples of this interaction between literary history and genre. In our own century, for instance, many pastoral topoi have been transferred into, and transformed through, the world of science fiction. Much of the description of Tralfamadore in Kurt Vonnegut's *Slaughterhouse-Five*, for instance, might have been lifted from a paean to a pastoral landscape, and another component of many versions of pastoral, unhampered sexuality, is abundantly present in Tralfamadore in the person of Montana Wildhack. It is suggestive that so many modern writers have chosen to locate pastoral ideals in a futuristic setting rather than in a past Golden Age and suggestive, too, that pastoral posits a timeless world (though one into which reminders of time may painfully intrude), while science fiction reshapes pastoral motifs in terms of the sense of rapid and unpredictable change that characterizes modern culture on so many levels.

When studying the relationship between generic evolution and literary history, we should heed the caveat offered by Tzvetan Todorov and many other critics as well: we should not expect the movement from one genre to another to follow a neat pattern. The image of the relay race suggested by some critics for generic evolution is apt in certain cases but not all. While a genre is still living it may compete with others that fill the same functions. Two genres may enjoy the relationship of genre and counter-genre while both are active, with one of the two taking over many elements of the other when it decays. The sonnet and the epyllion (an Ovidian mythological narrative) offer an intriguing and neglected instance of this type of relationship during the English Renaissance; while the two coexisted, the sexually aggressive women in the epyllia implicitly challenged the Petrarchan ideal, and the detached, wry epyllion speaker offered himself as an alternative to the melo-dramatic poet-lover in sonnet sequences. In certain cases more than one literary form may take over the functions of another form that has declined or died, with the estate being divided so slowly and complexly that the process makes Jarndyce vs Jarndyce, the labyrinthine case memorialized by Dickens, look simple by com-parison.

Applying principles like these will reveal certain unexpected family relationships. If, for example, we acknowledge that *épater le bourgeois* is one function of formal verse satire in the 1590s, then in this sense metaphysical poetry, even when it is wholly unsatirical, ranks as one of the heirs and assigns of that form of satire. Similarly, when the long poem declines in the seventeenth century the topographical poem assumes some of its subterranean roles – topographical poetry substitutes a geographical sweep, a spatial perspective, for the temporal one that characterizes many long poems, and it charts geological history in place of the dynastic history of epic.

As these instances might suggest, yet another challenge modern criticism faces is defining the functions of genres more thought-fully and more thoroughly than we have hitherto done. We need to approach the question as broadly as possible rather than confining ourselves only to obvious thematic functions (the sonnet serves to discuss love, the romance to celebrate chivalry and so on). We have, for example, observed that literary forms may perform a type of social function in that they establish their author's relationship to other writers: they may signal his respect for his predecessors or his contempt for them, as well as demarcating a small circle of writers from the larger literary culture with which they uneasily coexist. Some genres of course perform a social function in a more direct sense by providing a forum in which the poet can praise a patron or other social leader – and often a less obvious role assumed by such genres is to offer strategies by which the poet can praise someone or something without descending to sycophancy. Different though they may be in virtually every other way, Chaucer's *Book of the Duchess*, Jonson's 'To Penshurst' and Milton's *Comus* all rely on certain characteristics of their genres to flatter without appearing to fawn and, indeed, the literary forms in which Jonson and Milton are writing, the country-house poem and the masque, fulfill this function with particular frequency and skill.

One of the most significant functions of genre remains one of the most neglected. We should direct more of our current concern with 'literature as system' into a close study of how literary types interact with each other. Especially interesting are the habits of what might be termed host genres, those forms one of whose roles is to provide a hospitable environment for the other form or forms that are regularly incorporated within them. In some cases, for example, the host may assume the function of a screen, hiding or countervailing certain less desirable aspects of the genre within it. Thus the two literary types to which we just referred, the country-house poem and the masque, may both include satirical commentary on social evils in general or even on one aristocrat in particular, but the ways they distance their observations from daily reality, as well as their ostensible commitment to praise, help to screen their role as satires. Similarly, the epistle can mitigate both the harshness of formal verse satire and the imperiousness often associated with its speaker by suggesting his close relationship with the recipient, putative or actual, of the letter. And a complicated problem in the relationship of genre and counter-genre demands far more attention than it has received. Why do the two forms in question sometimes encourage each other's survival by providing a cross-current, an alternative to values in the other form that might seem totally unacceptable were they not somehow counterbalanced, and sometimes instead threaten each other's existence in the literary culture by their harsh mutual criticisms? When and why, in other words, does symbiosis turn to sabotage? Pastoral and satire suggest themselves as a useful test case.

The complexity with which genres act and interact invites us, then, to return to the psychological metaphor suggested in Chapter 1. A genre closely resembles a human personality in the way it may incorporate elements from many other personality types while still conforming to one basic type itself: someone whose fundamental configuration is obsessive may include elements of the depressive, much as a genre that is primarily epic may also participate in romance and pastoral. The biological analogy is less useful for this than many other aspects of genre. One could adduce hybrid animals – the Renaissance playwright Guarini does just that in trying to justify his experiments with a hybrid genre, tragicomedy – but both their rarity and their sterility render them less than ideal models for the admixture of literary types that often occurs within a genre, an admixture that can be very fertile in several senses of the word.

Genres resemble human personalities, too, in their complex relationships with those around them. They are, as we have often observed, shaped both by learning from and by rebelling against their literary parents, those earlier forms from which they develop. They may, too, maintain a tense and ambivalent relationship with those progenitors long after the parent genres cease to be in vogue, much as our emotional relationships with our relatives do not necessarily cease at their deaths.

In comparing personalities to genres earlier, we saw that a trait like aggressiveness may assume different forms in different person-alities. One might add that such a trait may also assume different forms within the same personality as it develops. Someone with an obsessive personality will probably not lose his concern for controlling and ordering the details of experience, but at various points in his life he may express that concern primarily by, say, cleaning his house with great energy or compiling a scholarly bibliography. Similarly, pastoral has a predilection for binary oppositions so fundamental that one suspects that if the genre did not exist the structuralists would have invented it – but that predilection may take the form of carefully articulated intellectual debates about city versus country, of rhetorical figures involving the comparison of opposites, or merely of one of the oldest binary oppositions, the debate between two lovers.

As these analogies would suggest, in studying generic patterns, like psychological ones, we always need to qualify our generalizations about the type with close and sympathetic observations about the individual human being or the individual work before us. For generic categories and principles rarely provide simple answers to problems about literature – but they regularly offer us one of the surest and most suggestive means of seeking those answers.

Select bibliography

This bibliography is necessarily very selective; in particular, the primary list is confined to works quoted in the text. Other useful bibliographies may, however, be found in Irvin Ehrenpreis, *The 'Types' Approach to Literature* and Paul Hernadi, *Beyond Genre*. The reader is also directed to two periodicals that regularly publish studies of genre, *Genre* and *New Literary History* (*NLH*), to the short-lived French journal *Helicon*, and to the volumes in the Critical Idiom series that examine particular genres.

Primary

Aristotle, *Aristotle's Theory of Poetry and Fine Art, With . . . The Poetics*, ed. and trans. S. H. Butcher, 4th edn, London: Macmillan, 1932.

Arnold, Matthew, *On the Classical Tradition*, ed. R. H. Super, *The Complete Prose Works of Matthew Arnold*, vol. I, Ann Arbor: University of Michigan Press, 1960.

Berryman, John, *Berryman's Sonnets*, New York: Farrar, Straus & Giroux, 1967.

Blair, Hugh, *Lectures on Rhetoric and Belles Lettres*, 2 vols, ed. Harold F. Harding, Carbondale, Ill.: Southern Illinois University Press, 1965.

Brunetière, Ferdinand, *L'évolution des genres dans l'histoire de la littérature*, 2 vols, 6th edn, Paris: Librairie Hachette, 1914.

Chaucer, Geoffrey, *The Works of Geoffrey Chaucer*, ed. F. N. Robinson, 2nd edn, Boston: Houghton Mifflin Co., 1957.

Coleridge, Samuel Taylor, *Coleridge's Miscellaneous Criticism*, ed. Thomas Middleton Raysor, Cambridge, Mass.: Harvard University Press, 1936.

Coleridge, Samuel Taylor, *Coleridge's Shakespearean Criticism*, 2 vols, ed. Thomas Middleton Raysor, Cambridge, Mass.: Harvard University Press, 1930.

Donne, John, *The Elegies and The Songs and Sonnets*, ed. Helen Gardner, Oxford: Clarendon Press, 1965.

Dryden, John, *The Works of John Dryden*, vol. XVII, *Prose 1668–1691*, Berkeley: University of California Press, 1971.

Eliot, T. S., *Selected Essays*, 2nd edn, New York: Harcourt, Brace & World, 1950.

Hall, Joseph, *The Collected Poems of Joseph Hall, Bishop of Exeter and Norwich*, ed. A. Davenport, Liverpool: Liverpool University Press, 1949.

Hawthorne, Nathaniel, *The Centenary Hawthorne*, vol. II, *The House of the Seven Gables*, ed. William Charvat *et al.*, Columbus, Ohio: Ohio State University Press, 1965.

Hegel, G. W. F., *Aesthetics*, 2 vols, trans. T. M. Knox, Oxford: Clarendon Press, 1975.

Hobbes, Thomas, 'Answer to Davenant's Preface to *Gondibert*', in *Critical Essays of the Seventeenth Century*, vol. II, ed. J. E. Spingarn, Oxford: Clarendon Press, 1908.

Horace, *Satires, Epistles, and Ars Poetica*, trans. H. Rushton Fairclough, Cambridge, Mass.: Harvard University Press, 1947.

Hugo, Victor, *Oeuvres poétiques complètes*, ed. Francis Bouvet, Paris: Jean-Jacques Pauvert, 1961.

Johnson, Samuel, *The Yale Edition of the Works of Samuel Johnson*, vol. VII, *Johnson on Shakespeare*, ed. Arthur Sherbo, New Haven, Conn.: Yale University Press, 1968.

Jonson, Ben, *Ben Jonson*, vol. VIII, *The Poems; The Prose Works*, ed. C. H. Herford and Percy Simpson, Oxford: Clarendon Press, 1947.

Joyce, James, *A Portrait of the Artist as a Young Man*, ed. Chester G. Anderson, New York: Viking Press, 1964.

Marlowe, Christopher, *The Jew of Malta*, ed. Richard W. Van Fossen, Lincoln, Nebr.: University of Nebraska Press, 1964.

Meredith, George, *The Poems of George Meredith*, 2 vols, ed. Phyllis R. Bartlett, New Haven, Conn.: Yale University Press, 1978.

Milton, John, *The Complete Prose Works of John Milton*, vol. I, New Haven, Conn.: Yale University Press, 1953.

Milton, John, *Complete Poetry and Major Prose*, ed. Merritt Y. Hughes, Indianapolis, Ind.: The Odyssey Press, 1957.

Petrarch, Francesco, *Petrarch's Lyric Poems*, ed. and trans. Robert M. Durling, Cambridge, Mass.: Harvard University Press, 1976.

Pope, Alexander, *The Twickenham Pope*, vol. I, *Pastoral Poetry and An Essay on Criticism*, ed. E. Audra and Aubrey Williams, London: Methuen, 1961.

Shakespeare, William, *Shakespeare's Sonnets*, ed. Stephen Booth, New Haven, Conn.: Yale University Press, 1977.

Sidney, Philip, *An Apology for Poetry*, ed. Geoffrey Shepherd, London: Nelson, 1965.

Sir Gawain and the Green Knight, trans. Marie Boroff, New York: Norton, 1967.

Spenser, Edmund, *The Works of Edmund Spenser, A Variorum Edition*, vol. VIII, *The Minor Poems*, vol. II, ed. Charles Grosvenor Osgood and Henry Gibbons Lotspeich, Baltimore, Md.: Johns Hopkins University Press, 1947.

Symonds, John, *Shakspere's Predecessors in the English Drama*, London: Smith, Elder & Co., 1884.

Wordsworth, William, *The Prose Works of William Wordsworth*, vol. I, ed. W. J. B. Owen and Jane Worthington Smyser, Oxford: Clarendon Press, 1974.

Wordsworth, William, *The Poetical Works of William Wordsworth*, 5 vols, ed. E. de Selincourt and Helen Darbishire, Oxford: Clarendon Press, 1940–9.

Young, Edward, *Conjectures on Original Composition*, ed. Edith J. Morley, Manchester: Manchester University Press, 1918.

Secondary

Babbitt, Irving, *The New Laokoon*, Boston: Houghton Mifflin Co., 1910.

Cites the abandonment of generic norms as a significant instance of aesthetic and cultural corruption.

Barthes, Roland, 'An introduction to the structural analysis of narrative', trans. Lionel Duisit, *NLH*, 6 (1975), 237–72.

Bloom, Harold, *The Anxiety of Influence*, London: Oxford University Press, 1973.

A presentation of the author's controversial theory of literary influence, which has many implications about genre.

Bloomfield, Morton W., 'Stylistics and the theory of literature', *NLH*, 7 (1976), 271–311.

Evaluates structuralist attempts to define genres.

Bovet, Ernest, *Lyrisme, épopée, drame*, Paris: Librairie Armand Colin, 1911.

Though published in this century, this is one of the most extreme examples of the nineteenth-century predilection for linking the evolution of genres to the evolution of societies.

Burke, Kenneth, *Attitudes toward History*, Los Altos, Cal.: Hermes, 1959.

Especially Chapter 2.

Colie, Rosalie L., *The Resources of Kind*, ed. Barbara K. Lewalski, Berkeley: University of California Press, 1973.

Colie, Rosalie L., *Shakespeare's Living Art*, Princeton, NJ: Princeton University Press, 1974.

Especially Introduction.

Crane, R. S., 'The concept of plot and the plot of *Tom Jones*', in *Critics and Criticism*, ed. R. S. Crane, Chicago: University of Chicago Press, 1952.

Croce, Benedetto, *Aesthetic*, trans. Douglas Ainslie, New York: Noonday, 1968.

Culler, Jonathan, *Structuralist Poetics*, Ithaca, NY: Cornell University Press, 1975.

Donohue, James J., *The Theory of Literary Kinds*, 2 vols, Dubuque, Iowa: Loras College Press, 1943, 1949.

A study of genre theory in classical antiquity.

Dubrow, Heather, 'The country-house poem: a study in generic development', *Genre*, 12 (1979), 153–79.

Ehrenpreis, Irvin, *The 'Types' Approach to Literature*, New York: King's Crown Press, 1945.

Part I includes a useful summary of genre theory in the late nineteenth and twentieth centuries; Part II examines the role of genre in high school and university curricula.

Eichenbaum, Boris, 'The theory of the formal method', in *Russian Formalist Criticism*, ed. Lee T. Lemon and Marion J. Reis, Lincoln, Nebr.: University of Nebraska Press, 1965.

One of the most important formalist essays.

Eliot, T. S., *The Three Voices of Poetry*, Cambridge: Cambridge University Press, 1953.

Posits three 'voices' related to but not necessarily identical with the three modes.

Erlich, Victor, *Russian Formalism*, 2nd edn, The Hague: Mouton, 1965.

A historical survey of the movement.

Fokkema, D. W. and Ibsch, Elrud Kunne-, *Theories of Literature in the Twentieth Century*, London: C. Hurst & Co., 1977.

Frye, Northrop, *Anatomy of Criticism*, Princeton, NJ: Princeton University Press, 1957.

A reader not previously familiar with Frye's terminology will find the glossary at the back of the book very helpful.

Frye, Northrop, 'The archetypes of literature', *Kenyon Review*, 13 (1951), 92–110, and in Northrop Frye, *Fables of Identity*, New York: Harcourt, Brace & World, 1963.

A useful distillation of many of the ideas Frye subsequently developed in *Anatomy of Criticism*.

Frye, Northrop, 'Myth, fiction, and displacement', *Daedalus*, 90 (1961), 587–605, and in Northrop Frye, *Fables of Identity*, New York: Harcourt, Brace & World, 1963.

Frye, Northrop, *A Natural Perspective*, New York: Columbia University Press, 1965.

Gombrich, E. H., *Art and Illusion*, 2nd edn, Princeton, NJ: Princeton University Press, 1961.

> The author's important observations on the visual arts are often equally applicable to literature; particularly relevant to genre are his analyses of the ways both the painter and the viewer are affected by pre-existing models and his allusions to Gestalt psychology.

Gombrich, E. H., *Norm and Form*, London: Phaidon, 1966.

Grabowski, Tadeusz, 'La question des genres littéraires dans l'étude contemporaine polonaise de la littérature', *Helicon*, 2 (1939), 211–15.

> Interesting on 'new' and sub-literary genres.

Guillén, Claudio, *Literature as System*, Princeton, NJ: Princeton University Press, 1971.

> Especially Chapters 3–6, 9.

Guillén, Claudio, 'Sátira y poética en Garcilaso', in *Homenaje a Casalduero*, ed. Rizel Pincus Sigele and Gonzalo Sobejano, Madrid: Gredos, 1972.

> Important study of the interrelationship of genres.

Guillén, Claudio, 'Literary change and multiple duration', *Comparative Literature Studies*, 14 (1977), 100–18.

Hamburger, Käte, *The Logic of Literature*, 2nd edn, trans. Marilynn J. Rose, Bloomington, Ind.: Indiana University Press, 1973.

Hathaway, Baxter, *The Age of Criticism*, Ithaca, NY: Cornell University Press, 1962.

> A study of criticism in the later Italian Renaissance.

Hernadi, Paul, *Beyond Genre*, Ithaca, NY: Cornell University Press, 1972.

> Useful summary of modern genre theory, to which the author adds his own formulation.

Hirsch, E. D., *Validity in Interpretation*, New Haven, Conn.: Yale University Press, 1967.

A hermeneutic approach to literary criticism, with some relevance to genre; in particular, the author's theory of 'intrinsic genre' is related to though distinct from genre in the customary senses.

Ingarden, Roman, *The Cognition of the Literary Work of Art*, trans. Ruth Ann Crowley and Kenneth R. Olson, Evanston, Ill.: Northwestern University Press, 1973.

A philosophical enquiry into the processes of cognition in relation to literature. Suggests a number of differences between the ways the reader perceives each of the three modes.

Jakobson, Roman, 'The dominant', in *Readings in Russian Poetics*, ed. Ladislav Matejka and Krystyna Pomorska, Cambridge, Mass.: MIT Press, 1971.

Jakobson, Roman, 'Linguistics and poetics', in *Style in Language*, ed. Thomas A. Sebeok, Cambridge, Mass.: MIT Press, 1960, and in *Essays on the Language of Literature*, ed. Seymour Chatman and Samuel R. Levin, Boston: Houghton Mifflin Co., 1967.

One of the most important essays in structuralist criticism.

Jameson, Fredric, 'Magical narratives: romance as genre', *NLH*, 7 (1975), 135–63.

Includes a number of suggestive theories about the nature of genre.

Jauss, Hans Robert, 'Literary history as a challenge to literary theory', trans. Elizabeth Bensinger, *NLH*, 2 (1970), 7–37, and in *New Directions in Literary History*, ed. Ralph Cohen, Baltimore, Md.: Johns Hopkins University Press, 1974.

Kohler, Pierre, 'Contribution à une philosophie des genres', *Helicon*, 1 (1938), 233–44, and 2 (1939), 135–42.

Argues that genres fill psychological needs for the author and reader.

Krieger, Murray (ed.), *Northrop Frye in Modern Criticism*, New York: Columbia University Press, 1966.

Lemon, Lee T. and Reis, Marion J. (eds), *Russian Formalist Criticism*, Lincoln, Nebr.: University of Nebraska Press, 1965.

Contains a number of suggestive essays on genre in addition to the major statement on the subject cited separately in this bibliography.

Lewalski, Barbara Kiefer, *Protestant Poetics and the Seventeenth-Century Religious Lyric*, Princeton, NJ: Princeton University Press, 1979.

Lewalski, Barbara Kiefer, *Milton's Brief Epic*, Providence, RI: Brown University Press, 1966.

Includes important research on Renaissance genre theory.

Lukács, George, *The Theory of the Novel*, trans. Anna Bostock, Cambridge, Mass.: MIT Press, 1971.

Lakács, George, *The Historical Novel*, trans. Hannah and Stanley Mitchell, Boston: Beacon Press, 1963.

Mantz, Harold Elmer, 'Types in literature', *Modern Language Review*, 12 (1917), 469–79.

Defends genre from Croce's attacks and describes forms as a kind of restraint on the artist's personality.

Matejka, Ladislav and Pomorska, Krystyna (eds), *Readings in Russian Poetics*, Cambridge, Mass.: MIT Press, 1971.

Like the Lemon and Reis anthology, this collection includes several essays relevant to genre in addition to the ones listed separately in the bibliography.

Minnis, A. J., 'Literary theory in discussions of *Formae Tractandi* by medieval theologians', *NLH*, 11 (1979), 133–45.

Minnis, A. J., 'Discussions of "authorial role" and "literary form" in late-medieval scriptural exegesis', *Beiträge zur Geschichte der Deutschen Sprache und Literatur*, 99 (1977), 37–65.

Mukarovský, Jan, *The Word and Verbal Art*, ed. and trans. John Burbank and Peter Steiner, New Haven, Conn.: Yale University Press, 1977.

Especially Chapters 3, 6 and 7.

Olson, Elder, 'An outline of poetic theory', in *Critics and Criticism*, ed. R. S. Crane, Chicago: University of Chicago Press, 1952.

Pearson, Norman Holmes, 'Literary forms and types; or, a defence of Polonius', *English Institute Annual 1940*, New York: AMS, 1965.

Pepper, Stephen C., *The Basis of Criticism in the Arts*, Cambridge, Mass.: Harvard University Press, 1945.

On 'funding', see especially pp. 70–3 and 148–71.

Poggioli, Renato, 'Poetics and metrics', in *Proceedings of the Second Congress of the International Comparative Literature Association*, vol. I, ed. Werner P. Friedrich, Chapel Hill, NC: University of North Carolina Press, 1959, and in Renato Poggioli, *The Spirit of the Letter*, Cambridge, Mass.: Harvard University Press, 1965.

Pomorska, Krystyna, *Russian Formalist Theory and Its Poetic Ambiance*, The Hague: Mouton, 1968.

A useful summary both of the principles of Russian formalism and of its intellectual and cultural roots.

Prusek, Jaroslav, 'History and epics in China and the West', *Diogenes*, 42 (1963), 20–44.

A thought-provoking study of an issue that has been unduly neglected: the relationship between western and non-western responses to genre. Also interesting on parallels between historiography and literary form.

Scholes, Robert, *Structuralism in Literature*, New Haven, Conn.: Yale University Press, 1974.

Trenchant presentation of structuralist principles; contains a useful summary and analysis of Frye.

Scholes, Robert and Kellogg, Robert, *The Nature of Narrative*, New York: Oxford University Press, 1966.

Staiger, Emil, *Grundbegriffe der Poetik*, 8th edn, Zürich: Atlantis Verlag, 1968.

Staiger, Emil, 'Time and the poetic imagination', *The Times Literary Supplement*, 27 September 1963, 747–8, and in *The Critical Moment*, London: Faber, 1964.

Convenient abridgement of some of the principles of *Grundbegriffe der Poetik*.

Todorov, Tzvetan, *The Fantastic*, trans. Richard Howard, Cleveland, Ohio: Case Western Reserve Press, 1973.

Especially Chapter 1.

Todorov, Tzvetan, 'The origin of genres', *NLH*, 8 (1976), 159–70.

Todorov, Tzvetan, *The Poetics of Prose*, trans. Richard Howard, Oxford: Basil Blackwell, 1977.

Tynyanov, Jurii, 'On literary evolution', in *Readings in Russian Poetics*, ed. Ladislav Matejka and Krystyna Pomorska, Cambridge, Mass.: MIT Press, 1971.

Van Tieghem, Paul, 'La question des genres littéraires', *Helicon*, 1 (1938), 95–101.

Viëtor, Karl, 'Probleme der literarischen Gattungsgeschichte', *Deutsche Vierteljahrsschrift für Literaturwissenschaft und Geistesgeschichte*, 9 (1931), 425–47.

Vivas, Eliseo, 'Literary classes: some problems', *Genre*, 1 (1968), 97–105.

Weinberg, Bernard, *A History of Literary Criticism in the Italian Renaissance*, 2 vols, Chicago: University of Chicago Press, 1961.

Especially Chapters 13, 19–20.

Wellek, René, 'Concepts of form and structure in twentieth-century criticism', in *Concepts of Criticism*, ed. Stephen G. Nichols, Jr, New Haven, Conn.: Yale University Press, 1973.

Wellek, René, 'The concept of evolution in literary history', in *Concepts of Criticism*, ed. Stephen G. Nichols, Jr, New Haven, Conn.: Yale University Press, 1973.

Very relevant to generic evolution.

Wellek, René, 'Genre theory, the lyric, and *Erlebnis*', in *Festschrift für Richard Alewyn*, ed. Herbert Singer and Benno von Weise, Köln: Böhlau Verlag, 1967, and in René Wellek, *Discriminations*, New Haven, Conn.: Yale University Press, 1970.

Wellek, René, *A History of Modern Criticism, 1750–1950*, 4 vols, New Haven, Conn., and London: Yale University Press, 1955–65.

Wellek, René and Warren, Austin, *Theory of Literature*, 3rd edn, New York: Harcourt, Brace & World, 1962.

Especially Chapter 17.

Whitemore, Charles E., 'The validity of literary definitions', *PMLA*, 39 (1924), 722–36.

Wimsatt, William K. and Brooks, Cleanth, *Literary Criticism*, New York: Alfred A. Knopf, 1962.

Index